Madagascar Hissing Cockroaches as pets.

Madagascar Hissing Cockroach book for pros and cons, housing, keeping, diet, care and health.

by

I0161860

Macy Peterson

Table of Contents

Introduction

I want to thank you and congratulate you for buying the book 'Madagascar hissing cockroach as a pet'. This book will help you to understand everything you need to know about domesticating a Madagascar hissing cockroach. You will learn all the aspects related to raising the Madagascar hissing cockroach successfully at home. You will be able to understand the pros and cons, behaviour, basic care, keeping, housing, diet and health related to the animal.

There are people who are impressed by the adorable looks of the Madagascar hissing cockroach. They think that this reason is enough to domesticate the animal. But, domestication of a Madagascar hissing cockroach has its unique challenges and issues.

If you are not ready for these challenges, then you are not ready to domesticate the animal. If you have already bought or adopted a Madagascar hissing cockroach, even then you need to understand your pet so that you take care of him in a better way. It is important that you understand that owning any pet will have its advantages and disadvantages.

You should see whether with all its pros and cons, the animal fits well into your household. Domesticating and taming a pet is not only fun. There is a lot of hard work that goes into it.

It is important that you are ready to commit before you decide to domesticate the animal. If you are a prospective buyer, then understanding of these points will help you to make a wise decision.

When you bring a pet home, it becomes your responsibility to raise the pet in the best way possible. You have to provide physically, mentally, emotionally and financially for the pet. Before you embark on this journey of raising your pet, it is important to evaluate your resources and make sure that you are ready for the pet.

You should also evaluate the practical side of things. It is important that you know that the cost of bringing up a Madagascar hissing cockroach might be more than the cost you would have to encounter while raising a dog or a cat.

It is important to have a thorough understanding about the animal. Spend some time to know everything about the Madagascar hissing cockroach. This will help you know your pet better. The more you know about your pet, the better bond you will form with him. Whenever you get a pet home, you have to make sure that you are all ready for the responsibilities ahead.

A pet is like a family member. This is the basic requirement to domesticate an animal. It is more than important that you take care of all the responsibilities for the animal.

If you wish to raise a Madagascar hissing cockroach as a pet, there are many things that you need to keep in mind. It can get very daunting for a new owner. Because of the lack of information, you will find yourself getting confused as to what should be done and what should be avoided. You might be confused and scared. But, there is no need to feel so confused. After you learn about the Madagascar hissing cockroaches, you will know how adorable they are. You should equip yourself with the right knowledge.

It is important that you understand the basic behaviour of the Madagascar hissing cockroach. This will help you to understand what is ahead for you. If you understand how a Madagascar hissing cockroach should be cared for, you will make it work for yourself. You should aim at learning about the animal and then doing the right thing for him. This will help you to form a relationship with him.

Once you form a relationship with the Madagascar hissing cockroach, it gets better and easier for you as the owner. The pet will grow up to be friendly and adorable. He will also value the bond as much as you do. This will be good for the pet and also for you as the pet owner in the long run.

If you are in two minds whether you need a Madagascar hissing cockroach or not, then this book will make it simpler for you. You should objectively look at the various advantages and disadvantages of owning a Madagascar hissing cockroach. This will help you to make your decision.

If you are looking to domesticate the Madagascar hissing cockroach, then you might be having many questions and doubts. You still might not be sure whether you want to buy the Madagascar hissing cockroach or not. If you are still doubtful, then this book is meant to help you make a well-informed decision.

This book is meant to equip you with all the knowledge that you need to have before buying the Madagascar hissing cockroach and bringing it home. This book will help you understand the basic behaviour and antics of the animal. You will also learn various tips and tricks. These tips and tricks will be a quick guide when you are looking for different ways to have fun with your pet. It is important that a prospective buyer has all the important information regarding a Madagascar hissing cockroach.

You need to make sure that you are ready in terms of the right preparation. This book will help you in this preparation and to be a better owner for your pet.

You will learn many ways to take care of your Madagascar hissing cockroach. This book will try to address every question that you might have when looking at raising the Madagascar hissing cockroach. You will be able to understand the pet and give it the care that it requires.

You can expect to learn the pet's basic behaviour, eating habits, shelter requirements, breeding, grooming and training techniques among other important things.

In short, the book will help you to be a better owner by learning everything about the animal. This will help you form an everlasting bond with the pet.

Chapter 1: Understanding a Madagascar hissing cockroach

Whenever a person thinks about keeping a pet, he would look for an option that is easy for him. Nobody would want a pet that is difficult to keep or is too much of a mess.

When it comes to keeping cockroaches at home, most people don't have the most favorable reaction. Some are scared of these harmless insects, while others think that these animals would be too much of a mess to keep.

The truth is far from this false belief. Most cockroach species are harmless to human beings. It is now known that these species don't even prefer living near the human areas.

It should be noted here that there are a few species that are harmful for human beings because they spread diseases. But most others including the Madagascar hissing cockroach are completely harmless.

These cockroaches live in woody areas and deserts. In the past twenty years, they have become popular as house pets. The reason behind this is that some enthusiasts kept these animals as pets and realized how simple and easy it is.

These cockroaches come in many shapes and sizes. They are very clean, contrary to popular belief.

It is also very cheap to raise these insects. This has encouraged many people to raise them so that they can serve as food items for other bigger pets. This serves as a cheaper option. There are many others that raise them to finally eat them.

1. What is a cockroach?

Let us start the book with an understanding of as what a cockroach is. This will help you to understand the Madagascar hissing cockroaches in a better way.

A cockroach is an insect that further has many species. It has six legs. These cockroaches can be of various shapes and sizes. A cockroach can be less than half an inch and can also be larger than three inches. These different shapes and sizes fall in different species of cockroaches.

If you have seen a cockroach, you will know that it is long in structure. The body is very sleek and narrow oval in its shape. It has a segmented body and also antennae. These antennae are very useful as they are used to discover and explore the world around the insect.

The cockroach has a great sense of smell. That is believed to be its real power or strength. It is much more advanced than the sense of smell of a human being. The cockroach can know of a food item from a fairly large distance because of this sense of smell.

The eyes of the cockroach are also fairly developed. The insect can easily distinguish light from dark. It can use this power to save itself from potential danger.

Cockroaches can also have wings. Different species have different kinds of wing structures. Some species have wings that are very translucent and are also fairly long. Some others have wings that are stubby and short. It should be noted here that some cockroach species have no wings at all.

Cockroaches need a constant access to a heat source. This is because they are cold blooded in nature.

2. In the wild

It is interesting to note that there are about 4000 species of various kinds of cockroaches. Though they have some common traits, you can expect the different species to show traits that are specific to their species.

There are some species that are found in the rain forests whereas many others like the desert areas. One thing that is common to most cockroach breeds is that they are very fond of dark spaces, which are little warmer or are humid.

These animals are nocturnal in nature. They could also be resting through the day. The cockroaches prefer to be in groups or clusters as they are called. They have simple family clusters. It should be noted here that many cockroach species could be exception to these.

There are many cockroach species that are pure herbivores. They will feed on simple food items. There are many species that are opportunistic feeders. Their food choice will depend on what is available.

Cockroaches are insect groups that are not considered to be hunters. They fall under the category of scavengers.

A cockroach has no problem feeding on food items that are left by other animals. The cockroach is okay with eating anything that it can find.

In the ecology, they play the role of a decomposer. They will help in decomposing leftovers and waste things. These species will also feed on rotten wood items.

3. Madagascar hissing cockroach

Gromphadorhina portentosa (Schaum) or the Madagascar hissing cockroach is known to be the native of Madagascar, which is the fourth biggest island in the world. Madagascar is situated off the east coast of Africa.

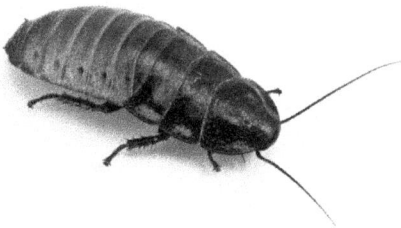

It is important that you understand the climatic conditions of the region. This will enable you to understand the favorable conditions for the Madagascar hissing cockroach. Understanding an animal's habitat and favorable climatic conditions is the first step to give the animal a happy and healthy environment at your home.

The climate of Madagascar supports different kinds of insects. In fact, there are various species of insects found in this island, even some of the largest insect species.

The climate of the region is sub-tropical to tropical. This allows the region to support many different kinds of flora and fauna.

The climate of the region is highly conducive to the Madagascar hissing cockroach.

The Madagascar hissing cockroach serves as food to many bigger animals at its native island. These animals include animals such as lizards, lemurs and birds.

A popular pet

The Madagascar hissing cockroach has gained a lot of popularity as a household pet in the recent times. For some people, this could be surprising as to how can a cockroach be a household pet, but this book will help you clear all your doubts. The Madagascar hissing cockroach will prove to be an excellent pet if all the necessary conditions are met.

4. Scientific classification

If you wish to study the classification of this animal scientifically, then the following information will help you:

Kingdom – The Animalia
Phylum – The Anthropoda
Class – The Insectaa
Order – The Blattodea
Family – The Blaberidae
Genus – The Gromphadorhini
Species – the G portentosa

5. Color of the Madagascar hissing cockroach

When you are planning to get a new pet home, it only makes sense that you understand every small thing about the pet. If you have seen a Madagascar hissing cockroach, you will know how it looks like.

If you have never seen a Madagascar hissing cockroach, this section will help you understand how the insect looks.

The insect is normally dark red in color. It can also have a black coloring. It is important to note here that the Madagascar hissing cockroach looks pretty much like the other cockroaches.

The color is pretty much the same. It is advised that you buy your Madagascar hissing cockroach from a certified breeder because many breeders can fool you by giving you an ordinary breed of cockroach.

6. Size

A Madagascar hissing cockroach reaches the size of 1.5 inches to 3 inches. This is the average size. There are reported instances where the Madagascar hissing cockroach has exceeded three inches in its size.

Weight

The weight of an adult Madagascar hissing cockroach is around 22.70 grams or 0.8 oz. This makes the cockroach very small and light weight.

7. Difference between the two sexes

The Madagascar hissing cockroach can either be a male cockroach or a female cockroach. It is important to understand the difference between the two sexes. This will also allow you to know whether your Madagascar hissing cockroach is a male or a female.

The male Madagascar hissing cockroach has two very big tubercles near the dorsal area of the prothorax. There are many people that mistake the tubercles as the eyes of the cockroach.

The head is situated below this area. The hard prothorax covers the head and provides protection.

The male has hairier and thicker antennae when compared to the antennae of the female cockroach. The horns of the male are big, which makes them stronger and attractive.

The tubercles of the male are not as smooth as the tubercles of the female. They are more prominent for the males.

8. Is Madagascar hissing cockroach a pest?

The Madagascar hissing cockroach is believed to be a pest by many people. This creates a fear in the minds of these people. How can you keep a pest as a pet at your home?

You don't have to worry as the Madagascar hissing cockroach is not a pest. You can be carefree when you are getting these insects home because they will not spread any bacteria or viruses.

The cockroach species, in general, is not believed to be a pest. These insects don't inhabit the human dwellings. They will always favor areas without human beings.

9. Madagascar hissing cockroaches as pets

It has been mentioned earlier that the Madagascar hissing cockroach makes an excellent pet. Though more and more people are keeping these animals as pets, there are many others who refuse to believe that insects can be kept as pets.

If you are also one of those people who don't believe that these insects can make excellent pets, then this chapter will help you to learn better.

If you are an owner of the Madagascar hissing cockroach or a potential one, even then this chapter will help you to understand these animals better.

The temperament of the Madagascar hissing cockroach is very docile. They can be aggressive, but that is only while they are in a fight with each other over a territory.

These animals can be handled very easily because of their soft and timid nature. You will face no difficulty when handling these insects.

Because these are unusual pets, there are many people who fear that they might harm the insect out of inexperience. You don't need to be afraid for this. The Madagascar hissing cockroach has a hard exoskeleton which gives the insect a good structure.

The exoskeleton makes sure that the insect is protected against external harm. You can lift the insect without the fear of harming the Madagascar hissing cockroach.

10. Life span

A Madagascar hissing cockroach has a life span of 2-5 years. But, there have been instances where Madagascar hissing cockroaches have lived longer than their average life span. The key is to provide them the right environment and also the right nutrition. This will help them to grow, stay healthy and live longer.

It is also important to note that Madagascar hissing cockroaches are susceptible to various disease causing viruses and bacteria. Once a Madagascar hissing cockroach gets a dangerous and life-threatening disease, it can be very difficult to cure him.

The pet Madagascar hissing cockroach will require you to pay a lot of attention to its health, be it vaccination or health care. The pet will definitely live longer if you make sure that you do all that is necessary for its health.

11. Madagascar hissing cockroaches in their natural habitat

In their natural habitat, the Madagascar hissing cockroaches will be found together in groups. Such groups of Madagascar hissing cockroaches are referred to as a business.

These Madagascar hissing cockroaches are opportunistic feeders by nature. They love their food and dwell on a good diet happily. It is known that earlier the Madagascar hissing cockroaches would eat only fruits. Their main food consisted of vegetables and fruits.

The Madagascar hissing cockroach has a very different digestive system. The digestive tract of the animal is very small. This arrangement has an effect on the food that the Madagascar hissing cockroach eats and the Madagascar hissing cockroach's health in general.

The Madagascar hissing cockroach has a high metabolism. While it can digest food faster than most animals, it can't digest many kinds of food. In its natural habitat, the animal is used to eating strictly meat.

The digestive system of the animal has accustomed to the habits of the animal since years. The digestive tract is not well equipped to digest all kinds of vegetables and plant protein.

A Madagascar hissing cockroach will have a scent gland. This will be located near the anus of the animal. The scent gland is used generally when the animal wishes to establish a territory.

They will also use it when they are scared of an impending danger. The release of the smell will be an attempt from the Madagascar hissing cockroach to scare off the thing that scares it. There is a chance that your pet might not be able to use its scent gland.

Generally, the Madagascar hissing cockroaches that are sold by the pet shops are neutered or spayed. Your breeder might also have neutered or spayed your Madagascar hissing cockroach. You should know that if the Madagascar hissing cockroach is neutered or spayed, then he would be unable to use the scent gland.

12. Breeding in Madagascar hissing cockroaches

A female Madagascar hissing cockroach will get sexually matured by the age of about four months. On the other hand, the male Madagascar hissing cockroach will reach sexual maturity when he is six to nine months old. If you wish to breed the Madagascar hissing cockroaches at home, then you will have to be prepared for this task.

You will be required to get your female and male Madagascar hissing cockroaches tested for their genes to establish whether they can be successfully mated or not. It is better to discuss this in detail with your vet.

If you are planning to breed your male and female Madagascar hissing cockroach at home, you should be on the lookout for the signs that show that the Madagascar hissing cockroaches are ready.

It is said that the first spring after a Madagascar hissing cockroach's birth is the season for its mating. The days will get longer and warmer during this time. The first tell-tale sign that the Madagascar hissing cockroaches are ready is that they secrete an odour and their skin become shiny because of the secretion of oil.

The female Madagascar hissing cockroach should be four months of age whereas the male Madagascar hissing cockroach should be at least six months of age. The female will have a discharge from her vagina and her vulva would also be swollen.

The male Madagascar hissing cockroach will be ready when his testicles enlarge and are visibly dropped from his body. The male will also use his oil and urine to mark his territory. You might even see him rolling in his own urine. Once you are sure that the female and the male are ready for mating, keep them in a single cage.

You should be ready to see some violent mating, which will not be a great sight. There will be a lot of dragging, wrestling and noise making. The male will bite the female over her neck so that she secretes her eggs.

The actual mating might take many hours or even many sessions. You should be prepared for this. This is normal, so there is nothing to worry or fret about.

After the process, keep them in separate cages and observe your female Madagascar hissing cockroach for signs of conceiving. The first sign will be that she will gain weight and will also pull her own fur from her body and tail. She will also make noises.

13. Bringing home a healthy Madagascar hissing cockroach

A major concern that many prospective owners and buyers of the Madagascar hissing cockroach have is how to make sure that the animal that they are getting home is healthy.

It is extremely critical that you get a healthy Madagascar hissing cockroach to your home because once you get an unhealthy kit you will only make things worse for yourself and the pet.

In the excitement of getting a new pet, you shouldn't forget the basic checks that you need to do before bringing the Madagascar hissing cockroach home. The last thing that anyone would expect after finding a breeder and getting an animal is that it is not in good health.

You will not know how to care for the sick pet. The pet's health will deteriorate. You will be spending thousands of dollars just on the health of the animal.

The following pointers will help you to make sure that your future pet is in the prime of its health:

-   It is very important to bring a healthy pet to your home. You should definitely avoid getting an injured animal home.

- Make sure that you learn as much as possible about the Madagascar hissing cockroach before you decide to buy him and bring him to your home.

- Even if the animal has had health issues in the past, it can be a matter of concern for you.

- A younger Madagascar hissing cockroach will have issues that could be different from an older Madagascar hissing cockroach. You need to make sure that you understand all these issues in detail.

- If you are buying an older Madagascar hissing cockroach, you need to be all the more vigilant because they could carry some infections.

- First and foremost, you should check the health care card of the animal that you wish to buy.

- All good breeders will maintain a health card, which will have all the details of past diseases and infections. This health card will also help you to understand the vaccine cycle of the animal.

- You will be able to understand which vaccines have been completed and which ones are due.

- It is always better to buy a Madagascar hissing cockroach whose vaccines have not been cancelled or missed.

- It is important that you closely examine your prospective pet. You should look for any abrasions on his skin.

- His skin should not be torn or bruised.

- You should make it a point to check the body temperature of the Madagascar hissing cockroach. The body temperature should be normal.

- If the Madagascar hissing cockroach is too cold or too hot to touch, then there is some problem with its health.

- You should closely look for any kind of injuries. If you find anything that does not seem normal, then you need to discuss it with the breeder.

- The Madagascar hissing cockroach should not have any broken limbs. You should be able to check this manually.

- You should look for any hanging limbs. A hanging head or limb could mean that the pet is severely injured.

- Also, carefully inspect the tail and stomach area also. There should be no abrasions.

- It is important that the Madagascar hissing cockroach is devoid of any infections or diseases when you bring him home.

- It is advisable to take the help of a qualified veterinarian to be sure of the kit's health conditions.

- He will be the best judge of his condition. A good vet will always guide you in the right direction for the Madagascar hissing cockroach.

- You should discuss at length about the concerns that you have regarding the Madagascar hissing cockroach.

- You should follow all the instructions that the doctor gives you because they will be for the benefit of the animal.

- You should only keep the Madagascar hissing cockroach if you are convinced that you will be able to care for the little animal.

- After you have brought the Madagascar hissing cockroach home, you should keep him isolated to keep an eye on him.

- You should allow him inside the house only after a few days of checking if everything is normal with the Madagascar hissing cockroach.

- In case of any issues, you should consult the vet and the breeder.

Chapter 2: Owning a Madagascar hissing cockroach

If you wish to own a Madagascar hissing cockroach or even if you already own one, it is important to understand the basic characteristics of the animal. You should know what you can expect from the animal and what you can't.

This will help you to tweak the way you behave with the Madagascar hissing cockroach in the household, which in turn will help to build a strong bond between the Madagascar hissing cockroach and you.

A pet is like a family member. You will be more like a parent than like a master to the pet. You will be amazed to see how much love and affection your Madagascar hissing cockroach will give through his ways and actions.

You have to make sure that the animal is taken care of. The animal should be loved in your household. If your family is not welcoming enough for the pet, the animal will lose its sense of being very quickly.

If the Madagascar hissing cockroach does not feel wanted and loved in your home, you will see a decline not just in its behaviour but also its health. This is the last thing that you should do to an animal. An animal deserves as much love and protection as a human being. You should be able to provide the pet a safe and sound home. Your family should be caring towards the pet. You have to be like a parent to the Madagascar hissing cockroach. This is the basic requirement when planning to bring an animal home.

All these points are not being discussed to frighten or scare you. In fact, these points are being discussed to make you understand that you have to know the right ways to domesticate a Madagascar hissing cockroach.

Madagascar hissing cockroaches are known to be very loyal animals. If they establish a trust factor with you, they will always remain loyal to you. This is a great quality to have in a domesticated animal.

Along with being loyal, they are also known to possess great intelligence. They will actually surprise you with their intelligence. This makes the pet all the more endearing.

They are also very entertaining and playful. You can expect the entire household to be entertained by the unique gimmicks and pranks of the Madagascar hissing cockroach.

In spite of all the qualities of the Madagascar hissing cockroach, it is often termed as a high maintenance pet. If you are still contemplating whether you wish to buy a Madagascar hissing cockroach or not, then it is important that you understand all about the maintenance of the pet, so that you can make the right choice for yourself.

1. Advantages and disadvantages of domesticating Madagascar hissing cockroaches

If you are in two minds whether you need a Madagascar hissing cockroach or not, then this section will make it simpler for you. You should objectively look at the various advantages and disadvantages of owning a Madagascar hissing cockroach. This will help you to make your decision.

It is important that you understand that owning any pet will have its advantages and disadvantages. You should see whether with all its pros and cons, the animal fits well into your household.

A few advantages and disadvantages of domestication of Madagascar hissing cockroaches have been discussed in this section. If you are a prospective buyer, then this section will help you to make a wise decision.

There are people who are impressed by the adorable looks of the Madagascar hissing cockroach. They think that this reason is enough to domesticate the animal. They believe that just because the pet is tiny, it wouldn't require any maintenance. But, this is not true.

Domestication of a Madagascar hissing cockroach has its unique challenges and issues. If you are not ready for these challenges, then you are not ready to domesticate the animal. Once you understand the areas that would require extra work from your side, you will automatically give your very best in those areas.

If you have already bought or adopted a Madagascar hissing cockroach, even then this section will help you. The list of pros and cons of Madagascar hissing cockroaches will help you to prepare yourself for the challenges that lie ahead of you. This list will help you to be a better parent to the pet and to form an ever-lasting bond with your beloved pet.

Advantages of domesticating a Madagascar hissing cockroach:

If you are still not sure about adopting or buying a Madagascar hissing cockroach, then you should know that there are many pros of domesticating a Madagascar hissing cockroach. They are loved by their owners and their families because of some amazing qualities that they possess. This animal can definitely prove to be a great pet for your household and your family.

The various advantages of domesticating a Madagascar hissing cockroach are as follows:

- The size of the Madagascar hissing cockroach makes it an ideal choice as a pet. They weigh only a few pounds, which makes them very light in comparison to many other commonly domesticated animals.

- Their looks make them adorable and cute to look at. They are loved by one and all. Who wouldn't want to have a pet that it beautiful to look at?

- They are very clean as contrary to popular belief.

- It is also very cheap to raise these insects. This has encouraged many people to raise them so that they can serve as food items for other bigger pets. This serves as a cheaper option. There are many others to raise them to finally eat them.

- When it comes to keeping cockroaches at home, most people don't have the most favorable reaction. Some are scared of these harmless insects, while others think that these animals would be too much of a mess to keep. The truth is far from this false belief. Most cockroach species are harmless to human beings.

- The temperament of the Madagascar hissing cockroach is very docile. They can be aggressive, but that is only while they are in a fight with each other over a territory.

- These animals can be handled very easily because of their soft and timid nature. You will face no difficulty to handle these insects.

- The Madagascar hissing cockroach has a hard exoskeleton which gives the insect a good structure. The exoskeleton makes sure that the insect is protected against external harms. You can lift the insect without the fear of harming the Madagascar hissing cockroach.

- The Madagascar hissing cockroach is larger in size when you compare it to other cockroach species. This also makes it easier to handle the Madagascar hissing cockroach. The larger the insect, the easier it is to handle it.

- Madagascar hissing cockroach is not a pest. You can be carefree when you are bringing these insects home because they will not spread any bacteria or viruses.

- There are many people that believe that housing an insect will be a very difficult task. People think that the conditions required for the Madagascar hissing cockroach would be difficult to maintain at a human house. But, this is not true. You would be happy to learn here that it is easy to house a Madagascar hissing cockroach. It is much simpler than housing many other popular house pets.

- People who love pets that can be lifted and cuddled will love the Madagascar hissing cockroach. A Madagascar hissing cockroach will allow you to lift it and play with it.

- This pet will be the centre of affection for all the family members and also for each and every visitor of the house.

- Madagascar hissing cockroaches are known to be very loyal animals. They will love your presence around them and will show you that they love you by their own unique ways.

- If they establish a trust factor with you, they will always remain loyal to you. Loyalty is a very good trait in an animal. This is a great quality to have in a domesticated animal.

- Madagascar hissing cockroaches are also known to possess great intelligence. You should be prepared to witness their intelligent antics and gimmicks. They will actually surprise you with their intelligence.

- A Madagascar hissing cockroach is a very sharp animal. It is always good to have a pet that is intelligent and sharp.

- These animals don't require a regular walk like many other pet animals.

- They are very entertaining. If you just sit around a Madagascar hissing cockroach, you are bound to have a great time.

- If there are kids in your home, then they will fall in love with this pet. But, you should monitor the interaction of the kids with the pet. This is important to keep everyone safe and sound.

- The Madagascar hissing cockroach is a very active and energetic animal when it is awake. It will keep itself happy and entertained. You will not have to worry much about the pet. In fact, this animal will be really fun to be around for all the family members. The Madagascar hissing cockroach will entertain you and your family with its antics.

- These pets sleep a lot. They will sleep most of the time, which gives you a lot of free time to do whatever you want to do.

- Everybody in the house will love the pet. This is because of its very unique nature. The Madagascar hissing cockroach will be very energetic, playful and happy kind of animal. They will play a lot, running from here to there in seconds.

- One of your main concerns could be the diet of the pet. Even if you love your pet dearly, you would want to avoid any hassles while feeding the pet. You might not have the time to prepare special food all the time. In case you domesticate a Madagascar hissing cockroach, then you will not have to worry too much about the diet. The Madagascar hissing cockroach can be served meat with some store bought Madagascar hissing cockroach food or kitten food.

There are easily available food items to ensure that the right nutrition is given to your pet.

- The Madagascar hissing cockroaches don't overeat, so you don't have to worry in this aspect. You can leave food in the container and the Madagascar hissing cockroach will eat as much is required. They are used to eating several small meals.

- A very important point to note here is that their demeanour will depend a lot on how they are raised. The preparation has to begin right from the start. You can't expect them to suddenly become friendly after years of wrong treatment. If they are raised to be social, they will be very social.

- The animal will secrete a gland that will make him smell when he is frightened and alarmed. But, if the pet is neutered or spayed, there will be no stinking and dirty smells. This can be a great relief for many people because who wants a pet who smells all the time.

- Madagascar hissing cockroaches live in groups in their natural environment. This makes them tolerant towards other Madagascar hissing cockroaches. The Madagascar hissing cockroaches will wrestle and play with each other. There is a very slight possibility that they will not get along.

- The Madagascar hissing cockroaches have a very good sense of smell. This quality helps them in evading danger and also helps them to get trained.

- Madagascar hissing cockroaches have a decent life, if they are taken care of. You can make a strong emotional bond with your pet and can enjoy the fruits of the bond for times to come.

Disadvantages of domesticating a Madagascar hissing cockroach:

While you have studied the advantages of domesticating a Madagascar hissing cockroach, it is also important to learn about the various disadvantages that come along. Everything that has merits will also have some demerits, and you should be prepared for this.

The adorable and friendly animal has his own set of challenges when it comes to domesticating them. It is important to understand these disadvantages so that you can be better prepared for them. Following are the disadvantages of raising a Madagascar hissing cockroach:

- The Madagascar hissing cockroaches are very energetic by nature. This behaviour could be difficult for a first time owner.

- The males are very aggressive to each other when it comes to marking their territory. They insects push one another to show the opponent how strong the insect is. It is not surprising that the roaches are capable of hurting each other. This makes it very important that too many male roaches are not housed together because this will create problems for the less dominant male roaches. It will also be unpleasant for your family to keep seeing the roaches fighting.

- The hissing cockroaches have padded feet which are so skilled that they can climb any surface. This makes it important that adequate precautions should be taken to prevent them from climbing and escaping.

- These animals have a very unique temperament, and it would require patience from your side to understand this kind of temperament.

- These animals sleep a lot. Though this can be an advantage for you, if you want a pet that will play with you all day, then you are in for a loss. The Madagascar hissing cockroach will play with you when it wants to.

- The Madagascar hissing cockroach can get hurt if it is too dark because of their weak eye sight.

- These animals are known to eat smaller but very frequent meals. So, you have to make sure that the Madagascar hissing cockroach has something to eat every 2-3 hours. Such maintenance could be difficult for some people.

- They get sick very easily. A lot of care has to be taken to ensure that they maintain good health.

- They catch disease causing bacteria and viruses very easily. Once infected, it is difficult to treat them.

- The Madagascar hissing cockroach has a habit to nip. This is a habit that helps them to interact with other Madagascar hissing cockroaches, but they can nip you also. Nipping can hurt you, but you can train the Madagascar hissing cockroach against such behaviour.

- The food that you serve them might be easily available, but the right brands might not be too cheap.

- They are definitely not suitable for someone who is looking for a quiet and calm pet. They are energetic, will run around and will also make noises.

- The Madagascar hissing cockroach can run from one place to another in a matter of seconds. A new owner might find it very difficult to keep track of this pet due to his over enthusiastic and energetic nature.

- Because of his energy levels, the Madagascar hissing cockroach can run into things and can get hurt very easily.

- The Madagascar hissing cockroaches are known to have very sharp teeth that can hurt small children. So, you need to make sure that the children are never left alone with the pet.

- They are so small that you can lose them if you don't keep track of what they are doing. This is very important.

- If the Madagascar hissing cockroach is lost, it is almost impossible to find it. He will not be able to find his way back to the house. And, the Madagascar hissing cockroach is so small that anything can happen to him when it is lost.

- The Madagascar hissing cockroach has a tendency to run into danger every now and then. You have to be very serious about Madagascar hissing cockroach proofing the house, else you will lose him.

- The animal seeks a lot of attention. The Madagascar hissing cockroach is a kind of pet that will require you to pamper him a lot.

- The pet can get stressed and depressed if he is left lonely for longer durations. You can't leave him in the cage for too long.

- You will have to spend a lot of money on the vaccination and healthcare of the Madagascar hissing cockroach.

- If spending too much money is an issue with you, then you will have to think twice before purchasing the animal.

- You should also understand the various other costs that you will encounter while raising your pet. You will have to spend a lot of money on their health.

- These animals love playing and running around. These pets are fond of exploring things. They can create a mess if not monitored.

2. Legal regulations

When you are studying the domestic Madagascar hissing cockroaches closely, it is important to understand the legal regulations that govern them. This will help you to know how easy it is for you domesticate the Madagascar hissing cockroach in your country.

- Australia: There are some places in Australia that allow the domestication of the Madagascar hissing cockroaches. The states may require you to have a legal license to domesticate them. There are some places where the keeping of these animals is illegal. For example, Queensland bans the domestication of Madagascar hissing cockroaches.

- United States: Previously, United States had banned the keeping and breeding of Madagascar hissing cockroaches. But, as the

Madagascar hissing cockroaches became popular in the late eighties and early nineties, the laws were changed for many places. Many places such as California still don't allow the domestication of Madagascar hissing cockroaches. Many military bases have banned the Madagascar hissing cockroaches in their areas.

You have to understand the licensing requirements in your area before you can keep a Madagascar hissing cockroach. This is important so that you can avert any future issues and problems. If you are looking to bring home a Madagascar hissing cockroach, then you should contact the animal shelter in your area. It is also recommended to look for a Madagascar hissing cockroach in an RSPCA rescue centre. You should make sure that before you make the payment and buy a Madagascar hissing cockroach, you understand all the legalities in your area. Your breeder will also help you to understand all the formalities that need to be done.

This is one of the most important steps while looking to domesticate a Madagascar hissing cockroach. You should make sure that you inform yourself well about this and speak to all the concerned and relevant people.

3. Things to know before you buy the Madagascar hissing cockroach

As a prospective owner, you might be wondering which costs you need to prepare for. You might also be thinking as to what is so special about bringing a Madagascar hissing cockroach home. Why should you be so prepared? Why isn't it like getting any other pet? To clear the various doubts in your head, you should understand the nature of the pet and also the various costs that you will incur while raising the pet.

Being well prepared is the best way to go about things. There are basically two kinds of costs that you will be looking to incur, which are as follows:

The one-time or initial costs: The initial costs are the ones that you will have to bear in the very beginning of the process of domestication of the animal. This will include the one-time payment that you will give to buy the animal.

There are other purchases that would come under this category. The initial costs that you will face when you have decided to domesticate a Madagascar hissing cockroach are the purchasing price of the animal, the permits and the license fee, the vaccines, purchasing price of food containers and the of the enclosure.

The regular or monthly costs: Even when you are done with the one-time payments, there are some other things that you won't be able to avoid. But, these finances can be planned well in advance. You can maintain a journal to keep track of them.

The monthly costs are the ones that you will have to spend each month or once every few months to raise the Madagascar hissing cockroach. This category includes the costs of the food requirements and health requirements of the pet. The various regular veterinarian visits, the sudden veterinarian visits and replacement of things come under the monthly category.

The various purchases you can expect

While you are all excited to domesticate the Madagascar hissing cockroach, you should also start planning for all that you can expect in the future while raising the pet Madagascar hissing cockroach. You can expect to incur the following:

Cost of buying the Madagascar hissing cockroach

The initial purchasing price of the Madagascar hissing cockroach could be higher when compared with the initial amount incurred in purchasing other regular animals. If spending money is an issue with you, then you will have to think twice before purchasing this animal. On the other hand, if spending money is not an issue then you should understand the other important factors for raising a Madagascar hissing cockroach and accordingly make a decision.

If you are planning to buy a Madagascar hissing cockroach from a pet shop, then you can expect to pay somewhere around $100/£77.62. In general, the Madagascar hissing cockroach can be anything from $65/£50.45 to about $250/£194.05.

But this is only the purchasing price of the Madagascar hissing cockroach; you will have to pay for the vaccinations of the animal also. These vaccinations could be anywhere between $100/£77.62 to 400 $400/£310.48.

You should make sure that you get the Madagascar hissing cockroach medically tested before buying it. The examination and tests will also add on to the initial price. You also have the option to adopt a Madagascar hissing cockroach. This will help you to avoid the initial purchasing price, though the other costs for raising the Madagascar hissing cockroach will remain essentially the same.

You should also understand that neutering and spaying the animal will additionally add on to the price. If the Madagascar hissing cockroach has already being neutered and spayed, the breeder will inform you about this.

Most breeders mark the neutered or spayed Madagascar hissing cockroaches by two dots near the ears. Good breeders will always make sure that the Madagascar hissing cockroaches that they are selling to you and other buyers are in the prime of their health.

They will take care of their vaccines and health in general. This again means that the breeder will charge more.

If your breeder has taken care of the initial doses of vaccines, then you should be fine with paying a little extra to this breeder because he has saved you from running here and there to get these important procedures done.

Cost of shelter

When you bring a pet home, you have to make the necessary arrangements to give it a comfortable home. The shelter of the animal will be his home, so it is important that you construct the shelter according to the animal's needs. If the pet is not indoors, then most likely he will be in his cage. If the cage is not comfortable, you will see your Madagascar hissing cockroach withdrawing from it. So, it is important to make this one time investment in a way that is best for the Madagascar hissing cockroach.

The Madagascar hissing cockroach will require a good quality and comfortable cage as its home. The Madagascar hissing cockroach will spend a lot of time indoors, so you should buy a good cage for the animal to rest and sleep.

If their shelter is not comfortable, the pet will be restless all the time. Even if you construct a very basic cage for the animal, it should have the necessary comfort.

This is a one-time cost, so you should not try to save money by keeping the pet's comfort at stake. The price of shelter will depend on the type of the shelter. You can expect to spend anywhere between $50/£38.81 to $500/£388.1 for the cage of the Madagascar hissing cockroach.

The cage should be accessorized well by you. The cage will require some basic stuff, such as bedding, hammocks and toys. The higher end cages will have tunnels to keep the pet occupied and happy.

These are the extra things that you will have to incur in addition to the basic price of the cage. This should be around $70/£54.33. Though they might not be necessary, these accessories will make the cage fun for the Madagascar hissing cockroach.

Cost of food

A domesticated Madagascar hissing cockroach will mostly be fed cat and kitten food. Madagascar hissing cockroaches are opportunistic animals, so it is important that they are served more food items apart from the basic kitten food. You might also have to include various supplements to give your pet overall nourishment.

This is a basic requirement of the pet that you can't evade. It is important that you understand the food requirements of your Madagascar hissing cockroach in the beginning, so that you can be prepared on the monetary front. This is important because if the animal does not get all the appropriate nutrients in the right amount, his health will suffer, which again will be an extra cost for you. So, make sure that you provide all the necessary nutrients to your pet animal. You should be prepared to spend about $20/£15.52 to $40/£31.05 on the diet of your pet every month. The will vary depending on various factors, such as the brand of products that you choose and also your exact location.

The kinds of food that you feed your pet will also affect the exact amount of food that you encounter per month. You should remember that the more lax you are regarding the money that goes into food, the more the amount of money that would go into health care will be.

If your pet is well fed, it will not fall sick that often. This will automatically reduce the amount of money that you would have to spend on the veterinarian and medication.

Cost of health care

It is important to invest in the health of a pet animal. This is necessary because an unhealthy animal is the breeding ground of many other diseases in the home. Your pet might pass on the diseases to other pets if not treated on time. This means danger for the pets and also the members of the family.

You will have to take the Madagascar hissing cockroach to the veterinarian for regular visits on his health. He will be able to guide you regarding any medications and vaccines that the pet may need. It is advised that for the very first year of domestication, you are extra careful regarding the health of the animal. You should also be prepared for unexpected costs, such as sudden illness or accident of the Madagascar hissing cockroach. Health care is provided at different prices in different areas. So, the veterinarian in your area could be costlier than the veterinarian in the nearby town.

You should work out all these things right in the beginning, so that you don't suffer any problems later. Realizing at a later stage that you can't keep the animal and giving it up is never a good idea. Madagascar hissing cockroaches can get sick very easily. You will have to invest in their health care. They are susceptible to many diseases such as respiratory infections and Adrenal diseases.

You should understand that taking care of these animals will require special skills. You should make sure that the veterinarian that you consult for your pet Madagascar hissing cockroach is experienced in handling such animals.

You should also be prepared to spend more money on their health than what you would have spent on other pet animals. It is believed that you should have an extra $1000/£776.2 saved for your Madagascar hissing cockroach's emergencies. He might require an operation or surgery because of a disease. You will have to spend money on getting the vaccines for the Madagascar hissing cockroach. These vaccines are critical to save the pet from diseases and deficiencies at a later stage, so make sure that you don't miss them.

The Madagascar hissing cockroach will require vaccines against rabies and some other diseases. There are many breeders that take care of the early vaccines of the pet before giving it to the new owners.

You should talk to your breeder regarding this. The breeder might include the money spent on vaccines in the final price that he might charge for the animal. You should also keep a track of the vaccines, so that you don't miss any.

Other costs

Although the main costs that you will encounter while raising your pet have already been discussed, there will be some extra things that you will have to take care of. Most of these are one-time costs only. You will have to spend money to buy stuff such as Madagascar hissing cockroach bedding, accessories, food and water bowls and toys for the pet.

You can expect to spend some $200/£155.24 on these things. The exact amount will depend on the wear and tear and the quality of the products. In order to keep a track of things, you should regularly check the various items in the cage of the pet.

If you think that something needs to be repaired or replaced, you should go ahead and do it.

4. Handling the Madagascar hissing cockroach

When you keep a pet, handling the pet is one of the main concerns in the minds of the owners of the pets. Nobody wants to buy a pet that can't be handled.

This section will help you to understand how you can handle your Madagascar hissing cockroach in the best possible way.

There are some cockroach enthusiasts that are just beginning their hobby to keep different kinds of cockroaches but are confused as to which ones to keep. The Madagascar hissing cockroach is the safest bet for them.

Such people should start from a relatively easier species such as the Madagascar hissing cockroach, and then move to other species. This is how simple it is to handle a Madagascar hissing cockroach.

There are many people who fear that they might harm the insect out of inexperience. You don't need to be afraid for this. Madagascar hissing cockroach has a hard exoskeleton which gives the insect a good structure.

The exoskeleton makes sure that the insect is protected against external harms. You can lift the insect without the fear of harming the Madagascar hissing cockroach.

The Madagascar hissing cockroach is larger in size when you compare it to other cockroach species. This also makes it easier to handle the Madagascar hissing cockroach. The larger the insect, the easier it is to handle it.

While it is easy to handle the Madagascar hissing cockroach, it does not mean that you can be extremely careless when handling the pet. You can't throw the pet here and there. You have to make sure that you are as careful as possible.

The Madagascar hissing cockroach is your responsibility, and you should be able to do everything to make sure that the Madagascar hissing cockroach is safe and sound in your care.

We will discuss some tips and tricks to make sure that the pet is safe when you are handling it. You should also make sure that all the family members understand the importance of handling a pet well.

If you are unable to do so, you can harm the pet. You can also scare the pet. He might get aggressive near you if he feels that he is not safe around you.

The following guidelines will come in handy while handling the Madagascar hissing cockroach:

- Make sure the kids of the family are not alone with the roach. Even if the kid does not mean harm, he can accidentally hurt the roach. This can be very serious for the insect. So, it is better that the children are accompanied by an adult when they are handling the roach.

- You should never startle the insect when he is resting on your hand. This can cause him to drop on the ground, which again can be very serious for the pet animal.

- When you are holding the roach in your hands, make sure that the grip of the hands is just right. You don't want your hands to be too tight or too loose. If the grip is too tight, you can hurt the pet insect and if it is too loose, the insect can drop from your hands.

- When you are handling the roach, make sure that the distance between the insect and the ground is not too much. This eliminates the risk of the insect falling very hard and hurting himself. This rule should be followed sincerely when you are still learning how to handle the roach.

- You need to be extra careful during the first few days when the pet is not used to you and you are not used to the pet. It is important to give each other time.

- Never apply too much force to pick up the roach. Be as gentle as possible. A sudden movement from your side can harm the cockroach.

How to pick up the roach?

It is important that you pick up the roach in an easy and comfortable way without stressing yourself and without hurting the roach.

You should spend some time in understanding the various body parts of the cockroach. This will help you to understand things in a better light.

To pick up the hissing cockroach, gently place your fingers around the thorax of the insect and lift it gently. The thorax is the section that is quite hard and is behind the head area of the cockroach.

Never apply too much force to pick up the roach. Be as gentle as possible. A sudden movement from your side can harm the cockroach.

5. Housing of the Madagascar hissing cockroach

Housing a pet is a very big responsibility. The animal needs to feel safe and comfortable. If you are unable to provide the pet with the same then you will only make the life of the pet difficult. This in turn will make your life difficult.

You should make all possible arrangements so that the pet gets all the necessary comfort in your home. Learn about the natural surroundings of the insect. This will help you to create a happy space for the animal.

There are many people that forget that a pet animal is a family member. Just like you would do everything to make the life easier for a family member, you should do the same for your pet animal.

The insect can't talk and ask you for all that it needs. You need to be proactive and do all that is possible to make the life of the pet easier.

There are many people that believe that housing an insect will be a very difficult task. People think that the conditions required for the Madagascar hissing cockroach would be difficult to maintain at a human house. But, this is not true.

You would be happy to learn here that it is easy to house a Madagascar hissing cockroach. It is much simpler than housing many other popular house pets.

This chapter will help you to understand what needs to be done to make sure that the pet is having a comfortable stay in your home. You will learn about all the dos' and don'ts that you need to follow.

Having said that, it should be noted here that you don't need to feel intimidated. A pet is kept in the home for joy. It is more than important that you maintain this joy while taking care of the pet.

Don't make the entire process a task. This will not help you or the pet. Rather, be happy and joyful and do all that needs to be done for the pet to be kept safe and healthy.

How to house more than one Madagascar hissing cockroach?

In their natural habitat, the Madagascar hissing cockroach is usually found in a colony. There are numerous colonies consisting of many Madagascar hissing cockroaches.

Because they are used to being in groups, you can easily house more than one Madagascar hissing cockroach in your home. The major problem is that you will have to get used to the hissing sounds of the roaches.

The Madagascar hissing cockroach is a social creature. It will display behavior that will make it suitable to live in groups. This is great for people who are looking to house multiple roaches.

If you are looking to house multiple Madagascar hissing cockroaches, there are few things that you need to keep in mind. The gender of the insects would need to be considered. You can't house them randomly because that can lead to many issues.

Housing multiple male roaches

The female cockroaches have a liking and attraction towards the dominant male members. Dominant male members in a territory tend to have a very loud and aggressive kind of hissing.

The males are very aggressive to each other when it comes to marking their territory. The insects push one another to show the opponent how strong the insect is.

It is not surprising that the roaches are capable of hurting each other. Many male roaches hurt each other while they are deeply engrossed in these kinds of territorial fights which are very aggressive.

This makes it very important that too many male roaches are not housed together because this will create problems for the less dominant male roaches. It will also be unpleasant for your family to keep seeing the roaches fighting.

It should be noted here that because the male members can fight over establishing a territory, it is not that the males should never be housed together. The less dominant one will lose but will not be severely harmed. You can expect a few cuts and bruises.

Housing multiple female roaches

If you wish to house multiple female roaches, then you should know that the female roaches are pretty docile to each other.

The female roaches don't indulge in fights to establish territory because that is the job of the male members. The females are social and easy going.

You can expect your female roaches to indulge in hissing from time to time. The hissing will not be as aggressive and loud as the hissing of the male roaches. It will be much softer.

The females can hiss alone or in a group as communal hissing. This shouldn't be very disturbing for you and your family, though it is better to be prepared.

These simple points should be kept in mind when you are looking to house multiple roaches in your home. You will not face too many problems when looking to house multiple roaches in your home.

Housing female and male roaches together

If you are thinking about housing female and male roaches together, then you can easily do it. The male and female roaches can co-exist happily.

This can particularly be a good idea if you are interested in the mating of the male and female roaches.

The female cockroaches have a liking and attraction towards the dominant male members. The males will fight over dominance with each other so that they can attract the female roach.

Dominant male members in a territory tend to have a very loud and aggressive kind of hissing. The weaker ones will not be able to show much power and will also hiss in softer tones when compared to the dominant male roaches.

Preventing escape of the roaches

It should be interesting to learn that the hissing cockroaches have padded feet which are so skilled that they can climb any surface. This makes it important that adequate precautions should be taken to prevent them from climbing and escaping. While you have placed your roach in a tank, you might be shocked when you see that your roach has comfortably escaped the tank. This is very much possible.

The padded feet of the hissing cockroaches enable them to climb even not so smooth surfaces. This needs be kept in mind while planning tanks and living spaces of the hissing roaches.

If the lid and the top of the tank has a little opening, the roach will slide away. Even if the tank has a very huge vertical distance, the roach will manage to cover the distance.

There have been many escaping incidents of the hissing roaches. Once they escape, it can be very difficult to get them back because they will run away to another place in a matter of seconds. The size of the hissing roach also serves as a hindrance when trying to locate them. It is a benefit for them when they are trying to escape. They can squeeze in through the tiniest of gaps.

It is important that when you are planning the habitat of the insect, you do your research well. It is important to learn from the mistakes of other hissing cockroach owners so that you don't repeat the same mistakes.

If you know such people you should speak to them before you finalize the design of your pet home.

You should also visit various pet shops to understand what will work for you and what won't. This will enable you to create the best possible living space for your pet insect.

Chapter 3: Decoding the Madagascar hissing cockroach's hissing and other behaviour

A Madagascar hissing cockroach is a small naughty animal that will keep you busy and entertained by all its unique antics and mischiefs. It is said that each animal is different from the other. Each one will have some traits that are unique to him.

While you will learn about all the unique traits that your particular Madagascar hissing cockroach has by experiencing him and spending time with him, there are some traits that almost all Madagascar hissing cockroaches will exhibit.

It is beneficial to know of these traits so that you are not taken off guard. You will be able to understand what is normal for this animal and what is not. This will help you to be more prepared and not be confused every time something happens.

It is important to understand the behaviour and temperament of the specific animal that you wish to domesticate. This will help you to be a better master. Your Madagascar hissing cockroach might still have some surprises for you, but it is better to know of the general behaviour of the animal.

Understanding the behaviour will also help you to understand the Madagascar hissing cockroach's behaviour with other animals. You will be able to understand whether your Madagascar hissing cockroach will be friendly with other pets in your home.

1. Understanding the behaviour of the Madagascar hissing cockroach

It is important that you understand the various criteria that will affect the compatibility of various pets with each other. The given points will help you to understand factors on which the compatibility of various pets depends. These points will help you to plan how you can keep your different kinds of pets together.

The following personality traits will help you to be better prepared for your pet Madagascar hissing cockroach:

Wrestling

If you are planning to domesticate more than one Madagascar hissing cockroach, then this is one antic that you will notice a lot in your Madagascar hissing cockroaches. Madagascar hissing cockroaches love to wrestle with each other. Actually, Madagascar hissing cockroaches are very joyful and playful. But, they can be very rough with each other while playing. It might appear more like they are wrestling than playing.

The dominant Madagascar hissing cockroach will try his antics on the poor submissive one. You will find them making sounds of excitement. Don't worry because this is a very normal behaviour in Madagascar hissing cockroaches. But, do keep an eye on the Madagascar hissing cockroaches so that things don't get out of hand.

Rolling

This is a special kind of roll in which a Madagascar hissing cockroach holds another Madagascar hissing cockroach by his loose skin and rolls him over. This is a very common trait in Madagascar hissing cockroaches. If you are planning to have more than one Madagascar hissing cockroach at your home, you can expect to witness a lot of alligator rolls.

This technique is basically a way of establishing supremacy for a Madagascar hissing cockroach. A strong and dominant Madagascar hissing cockroach will get hold of the loose skin at the back of the submissive Madagascar hissing cockroach and roll him. There is nothing to worry because such flips are generally not harmful and the Madagascar hissing cockroaches are just being playful.

If a Madagascar hissing cockroach is alone, he might just flip and roll on the floor to show that he is happy and playful. You should worry if the Madagascar hissing cockroach tries to try this on you. He might try to get hold of loose skin on you and might try to nip you and bite you. This can be painful for you. But, you should know that this is a very normal thing for a Madagascar hissing cockroach and that you can nip train him.

Spotting a scared cockroach

It is easy to spot a scared Madagascar hissing cockroach. If you see your Madagascar hissing cockroach being pushed up in a corner, you should know that something is not right. If he is making noises similar to a hiss then you should know that he is definitely scared.

It is important to know when your pet is scared so that you can comfort him and make him feel better. There are different ways to comfort different kinds of animals. For your Madagascar hissing cockroach, you just need to let him be.

Leave the pet alone, but be in the vicinity so that you can keep a check on him. The Madagascar hissing cockroach is known to recover on its own. He will know when the danger that frightened him is no longer there, and this will help him to get back to normal. If you really wish to help then speak a few kind words to your pet.

Don't make the mistake of taking him in your arms. This is not required right now. Just speak a few kind words to reinforce the fact that everything is fine and then just leave the Madagascar hissing cockroach for some time. This works for a scared Madagascar hissing cockroach.

It should also be noted here that there is another reason for a Madagascar hissing cockroach to curl into a corner. This could also mean that the Madagascar hissing cockroach wants to defecate. If you see your Madagascar hissing cockroach tucked up into a corner, look out for whether he is scared or not. If you don't hear him making noises or acting all scared, then this means that he wants to defecate.

As soon as you have established that this is the reason for your pet to be in the corner, you should take him to a litter box. It should be noted that if you don't act immediately, your pet will defecate on your floor or carpet. He will not wait for you to act, so you need to be quick.

Dancing

Dance of joy a very popular and endearing trait of the Madagascar hissing cockroach and is its dance of joy. When a Madagascar hissing cockroach is all excited, he will jump and flip. He will do everything that sounds crazy. He will dart from one side to another. You might see him jumping off the top of furniture.

The Madagascar hissing cockroach might also emit certain kinds of sounds during this dance of joy. This is a simple indication for you that the pet is very excited and happy and wants to play and have some fun with you.

A new owner might not take well to this unique way of displaying excitement. There are many owners and their family members who get scared after seeing the Madagascar hissing cockroach like this. But, you should know that this behaviour is completely normal and the Madagascar hissing cockroach will not harm you. He is just having fun and wants to include you in his fun.

Chasing

Game of chase is one of the most favourite plays of the Madagascar hissing cockroaches. If you have more than one Madagascar hissing cockroach, you will often see them chasing each other. The pet will also try to get the attention of the owner either to chase him or to get chased by him.

Many new owners get scared when they see their pet all excited running around them. There is nothing to worry because the pet is only trying to start a game of chase with you. You can take a long cloth such as a blanket or towel and run with it. Your Madagascar hissing cockroach will happily run after you.

If you are the one who is chasing the Madagascar hissing cockroach, then make sure that you maintain a good distance between you and the animal because these animals have another unique trait. The Madagascar hissing cockroach might just suddenly stop while running. If you are not careful, you might just trample your pet Madagascar hissing cockroach, which is the last thing that you would want to do with your pet.

Biting

Madagascar hissing cockroaches have a tendency to nip. You should know that this is absolutely normal for a Madagascar hissing cockroach and that you can slowly train the Madagascar hissing cockroach not to exhibit such behaviour. It is important that you understand that reason behind a Madagascar hissing cockroach's nipping. You should not harm the pet when he nips. This could scare him and will make things worse for you.

More often than not, Madagascar hissing cockroaches do so when they are in a playful mood. If your Madagascar hissing cockroach wants you to play with him, he could just signal you to do so by nipping. Such behaviour is quite common in younger Madagascar hissing cockroaches. So, don't be surprised when the young Madagascar hissing cockroach nips really hard.

Nipping comes very naturally to the Madagascar hissing cockroaches. In their natural environment, Madagascar hissing cockroaches are known to nip each other. But, this does not harm them because of the quality of their skin. If you notice the skin of your pet, you will find it to be very thick. This thick skin is a cushion for the Madagascar hissing cockroach.

Another reason behind a Madagascar hissing cockroach's nipping is that the animal could be scared. When you bring the pet to your home for the first time, everything around him will be new. It is quite natural for the pet to get scared. This is the reason that nipping is very common in a new pet Madagascar hissing cockroach.

Scratching

You will also catch your Madagascar hissing cockroach scratching itself multiple times. As a new owner, this could bug you. But, you should know that this is a very normal behaviour. The skin of the Madagascar hissing cockroach is such that it can get itchy and the pet might have to scratch.

Though scratching is normal and nothing worrisome, if there are other symptoms that accompany it, then you need to see a vet. If the skin is red and shows abrasions, then this could be an allergy. You need to check with the vet to understand the condition.

The animal also has a tendency to catch fleas. If you spot fleas on the animal, don't ignore it. You can make use of anti-flea products for the pet and should consult the veterinarian if the symptoms persist.

Hiding

You might also find your Madagascar hissing cockroach hiding certain stuff. The thing with the Madagascar hissing cockroach is that they can get obsessed with certain things. For example, if there are ten toys in the Madagascar hissing cockroach's cage, he might get too attached to a couple of them.

If he gets obsessed with something, he will not chew on it or harm it but will look for places to hide that thing. He might hide his favourite shirt or toy in a place where he feels that it is safe.

Another thing with these pets is that they will not like you or anybody getting close to that object. For example, if you find out the hiding place of the Madagascar hissing cockroach's favourite toy and take it out from there, he will get very angry also stressed. So, you should definitely avoid giving your pet this kind of stress.

Your job should be to make sure that they are hiding stuff that is safe for him and not too relevant for you. You can't allow the pet to hide a knife or cupboard keys. Always know what the pet is up to, so that he can't come up with something dangerous.

Make sure you don't let them get obsessed with such things. Break the obsession right in the beginning, so that the pet can look for a new thing to get obsessed with and hide.

2. Madagascar hissing cockroach's hissing

The Madagascar hissing cockroach is known to produce hissing sounds. It is important to learn about these particular sounds so that you don't feel surprised when the insect makes these sounds.

It is important to note that the only species of insects to make hissing sounds is the Madagascar hissing cockroach. No other insect is known to make these kinds of sounds, though these insects can produce other kinds of sounds.

It is known that most insects that are able to produce sounds are able to do so by rubbing various parts of their bodies. Such sounds are very different from the hissing sounds that are being discussed here.

The different kinds of hissing sounds made by the Madagascar hissing cockroach are:

Fighting hiss

Fighting hiss is a kind of hiss that the Madagascar hissing cockroach produces. The male members are known to fight with each other to establish their territory. While doing so, they produce this particular kind of hiss.

The males are very aggressive to each other when it comes to marking their territory. They insects push one another with the help of horns. They also push very hard. This is done to show the opponent how strong the insect is.

44

It is not surprising that the roaches are capable of hurting each other. Many male roaches hurt each other while they are deeply engrossed in these kinds of territorial fights which are very aggressive.

Both the parties involved in these kinds of fights hiss from time to time. It should be noted that the roach that is more dominant or the one that is winning is the one that hisses more than the other one.

The fighting hiss can be said to be a hiss of dominance. The dominant Madagascar hissing cockroach hisses more and often in a louder tone to tell everyone that he is winning the battle.

Mating hiss

Mating hiss is also a kind of hiss that the Madagascar hissing cockroach produces. The members, when mating with each other, produce this particular kind of hiss. In fact, hissing is a very important ritual or part of the entire mating process.

It should be noted here that the female roaches also hiss during the mating procedure, but the hissing is mostly done by the male roaches.

The female cockroaches have a liking and attraction towards the dominant male members. Dominant male members in a territory tend to have a very loud and aggressive kind of hissing.

The males are very aggressive to each other when it comes to marking their territory. The insects push one another to show the opponent how strong the insect is.

It is not surprising that the roaches are capable of hurting each other. Many male roaches hurt each other while they are deeply engrossed in these kinds of territorial fights which are very aggressive.

Both the parties involved in these kinds of fights hiss from time to time. It should be noted that the roach that is more dominant or the one that is winning is the one that hisses more than the other one.

The dominant Madagascar hissing cockroach hisses more and often in a louder tone to tell everyone that he is winning the battle. The female

Madagascar hissing cockroach will be attracted to such strong male members.

A loud hiss will help a male roach to attract a female roach. If the roaches mate, the male will also hiss regularly during the mating process.

Disturbance hiss

There is a lot of debate surrounding the disturbance hiss that is produced by the Madagascar hissing cockroaches. The experts are still trying to find out the exact causes of the disturbance hiss.

According to what is already known, the disturbance hiss is produced by Madagascar hissing cockroach for various reasons.

This kind of hissing sound is produced by both the females and the male cockroaches. It is also believed to be an anti-predatory technique. The roach is believed is believed to make this hiss sound when it encounters something that can turn out to be dangerous for the Madagascar hissing cockroach.

This survival technique helps the roach to protect itself from potential danger, though there is little evidence of the same.

Communal hiss

If you are planning to have more than one Madagascar hissing cockroach in your home, then you can expect hissing sessions from all of them where they hiss together in unison. There can be various reasons as to why the Madagascar hissing cockroaches hiss together, most reasons are still under debate by the experts.

If Madagascar hissing cockroaches are housed together, they will try to establish a hierarchy in their establishment. This is a must for the Madagascar hissing cockroaches.

Hissing comes as a helpful technique while trying to establish a hierarchy of who is more dominant.

The experts and handlers of these roaches believe that there could be other reasons such as expressing joy or other emotion that could be the reason for hissing.

If you are planning to have more than one Madagascar hissing cockroach in your home, you need to be prepared for the hissing sessions. There is no point in being surprised later because this is something that comes very naturally to these insects.

If you are not comfortable with too many Madagascar hissing cockroaches hissing together then either house them separately or buy less number of roaches.

It is important that you are prepared for the communal hissing of the Madagascar hissing cockroaches. There is no way you can stop them from doing this so better be equipped in the best way possible.

Chapter 4: Setting up the Madagascar hissing cockroach's home

This chapter is an attempt to help you understand the importance of a shelter or a cage in an animal's life. You will be able to understand the basic concerns while building the cage for the Madagascar hissing cockroach.

Domesticating a cockroach requires a lot of planning. You can't buy one from the store and domesticate it without a proper plan because that won't work for you.

It is always advised to read more and more about the subject to get yourself acquainted and fully prepared. To make things smoother for you, it is a better idea to start with animals that are easier to keep.

There are many people who have managed to keep a roach without any prior experience of insect life. It completely depends on you and your choice. Just be aware of the pros and cons of both.

While it is important to have a cage, it is also important that the cage is of the right size. The advisable dimensions and specifications of the cage have also been listed. This will help you to build or a get a cage that is most suitable for your pet.

Like you need a home, an animal also needs a place and space that he can call his home. A home should make him happy and should be inviting for him. When the home does not provide the comfort and security that it should, it can lead to detrimental results.

There are many owners who might feel that there is no need to set up a cage because the pet can stay indoors. But, you need to remember that even if you are a hands-on parent of the pet, there will be times when the pet would be unsupervised.

There will be times when you will have to concentrate on some other work and the Madagascar hissing cockroach would be alone. The cage is very handy at such times because you can do your work and can also be sure that you pet is safe and sound in the cage that you have built for him.

Also, during the night time, it is best for the pet and also for the family members that the pet sleeps in his cage. The pet will get used to the cage and your family members can also sleep without any tensions of your pet being loose in the house.

1. Building the right enclosure

If you are looking at the measurements of the cage then a cage of two feet height and three feet width is suitable for a Madagascar hissing cockroach. This kind of a cage is suitable for up to three Madagascar hissing cockroaches. The type of cage you have will directly affect the physical health and mental health of your pet Madagascar hissing cockroach.

When you are building a cage for the Madagascar hissing cockroach, you have to make sure that you have provisions for the most basic and important things, such as food and water. The ideal cage will be spacious enough. It will allow the animal to roam around freely and rest well when it wants to.

You can use two big containers for food and water. It is important that the pet has access to food and water at all times. You don't want to be busy somewhere else when your pet is stressed with the lack of water.

While you make sure that food and water is available to the pet, you also have to make sure that the containers are not movable. The Madagascar hissing cockroach, owing to his natural tendency, might just kick the containers without realizing that the food and water in them was important for him.

To make things easier for you and the Madagascar hissing cockroach, you can attach the food and water containers to the cage. You will easily get the tools to do so. When you attach the containers, the Madagascar hissing cockroach can't move them. This will also help you to keep the cage clean and mess free.

The bedding that you choose for the Madagascar hissing cockroach should be comfortable. It should not occupy the entire cage because your pet needs some space to roam around also. You can get the right bedding for your pet Madagascar hissing cockroach from a pet store that sells Madagascar hissing cockroach products.

The best buy for a cage is the one that can be cleaned easily. The cage should be comfortable and fun for the pet, but also easy to clean for you. You can go for a cage that has a bottom made of plastic and also coated wire. Such bottoms can be lifted for cleaning purposes.

But, make sure that the wire can't be chewed by the pet Madagascar hissing cockroach. You can also go for the metal bottomed cage, but you need to be extra careful with these kinds of cages. You will have to make sure that such cages are not exposed to faeces and urine, otherwise they will rust. You can buy mats and rugs that are can be thrown after use to cover such bottoms.

A very important tip that you should always remember is that the cage bottom should not be covered with pine chips or cedar chips. These chips have certain oils that can cause damage to the liver of the animal and can also affect his respiratory system.

You might have seen Madagascar hissing cockroaches being on display in a shop in a cage with pine chips or a glass aquarium with the chips. But, if you wish to keep your Madagascar hissing cockroaches healthy and happy, both the glass boxes and pine chips should be avoided. The simplest cage that you can build for your pet is a cage with fixed food and water containers and mats over wire mesh flooring.

You should also keep the food and water containers on opposite sides. The Madagascar hissing cockroach would not want to defecate at a place where he eats food. You should also try to keep a hanging bottle of water along with the water bowl. This hanging bottle can be hung to the cage door.

While getting the cage made up, you should remember that a certain amount of privacy is needed by the pet Madagascar hissing cockroach. This is important so that the Madagascar hissing cockroach can be healthy at a mental level.

If the Madagascar hissing cockroach does not get what it wants, the pet will get stressed and might withdraw from you. There should be darkness in the cage when the Madagascar hissing cockroach is fast asleep. You can even cover the top of the cage with a sheet or a blanket to make it really dark and secure for the pet Madagascar hissing cockroach.

It is important that the bedding of the pet is soft and comfortable so that he can slide in and feel comfortable. But, make sure that you check the bedding every day to know whether the pet Madagascar hissing cockroach has been chewing on its material. This can be dangerous so you need to replace such items.

If you wish to keep two or more Madagascar hissing cockroaches in the house, then your cage requirements will automatically be changed. You can keep the Madagascar hissing cockroaches in separate cages. If the Madagascar hissing cockroaches get along, you can also keep them in a single cage.

You should make sure that the single cage is comfortable for both the animals. There should also be some additional space for the second Madagascar hissing cockroach in the cage.

Though the Madagascar hissing cockroaches are very small in size, they need to be comfortable in their shelter. It should be noted that you need additional space per animal in the cage. If you are planning to keep more than one Madagascar hissing cockroach, then you should plan the additional space accordingly.

It is not advisable to keep too many Madagascar hissing cockroaches in a single cage because not all of them get along with each other. So before you plan the cage, make sure that you know how many animals would be sharing the space. This will help you to keep the right amount of additional space.

Keeping a tank

You can keep the roach in an aquarium tank, without keeping any water in it. The first step when you are planning to buy a roach is to get an aquarium. And, the next step in preparing an aquarium is to understand the size requirements of the aquarium.

It should be noted that the size of the aquarium directly depends on the size and species of the roach. The various species have different requirements.

If you already have a fish aquarium in your home, you can convert the same into a tank for the roach. You would have to take certain precautions for the same.

You should also remember that there are no rights and wrongs here. Though it is advised to start with relatively easier insects, this does not mean that you can't keep a Madagascar hissing cockroach right in the beginning.

There are many people who have managed to keep roaches without any prior experience of insect life. It completely depends on you and your choice. Just be aware of the pros and cons of both.

In any case you have to take some preparations before you can keep an insect. This chapter will help you with an equipment list that will allow you to prepare the tank for the new insect that you will bring to your place. Proper care is of utmost importance for the pet invertebrate.

It is known that many insects lose their lives because of the lax attitude of their owners. If you are not careful, you will only lose your pet.

If you don't have any experience of keeping an insect, then you need to understand this step very well.

It is very important to make sure that the tank is closed properly because a cockroach will escape from any hole or outlet that he finds. There are many ways to make sure that your tank is escape proof. This chapter will help you to understand those ways.

Improper equipment can kill an animal. If you are a novice when it comes to keeping an insect then you need to pay all the more attention to this step. A small error on your part can kill the poor animal.

There are many people that want to keep an insect at home. The first question that bothers these people is how they will manage to keep the right environment in the tank. This will require consistent efforts from your side, but in turn you will be able to keep your cockroach happy and healthy.

Material

When you go to buy or install a tank, you will have to decide on the material of the aquarium or tank. This is an important decision because this will have a long term effect on the keeping of the animal.

It is suggested that you opt for a glass aquarium or acrylic aquarium. These are the usual aquariums that you will find in most stores that house marine life in water tanks.

2. Accessories

Besides the basic stuff, such as food and water, it is also important to accessorize the cage well. This is important because the right accessories will help him to feel like he is at home. They will bring him closer to his natural habitat and natural tendencies.

When you are planning the furnishing and accessories of the shelter, then you should make sure that you give the pet an environment that closely resembles his natural habitat. This will keep him happy and spirited. And when the pet is happy, then everything around is good.

When you are looking to place the bedding in the cage, you should remember that the Madagascar hissing cockroach has a natural tendency to create and form burrows. He would want something that will help him to emulate the action of digging. There are several accessories available these days that will help you to keep your Madagascar hissing cockroach happy.

When you bring a pet home, the pet will be scared of the new surroundings. You will have to make all the attempts that will help the pet to adjust in the new environment.

One of the safest ways to welcome a new pet is to provide him with a good shelter. The shelter should be as comfortable as possible. While you might save money of buying a cheap cage, you need to understand what is important.

The pet is more like a new member in the family, a new baby in the house. So when you buy the animal, you should make sure that you understand the needs of the animal at various stages of his life.

It is better to spend some extra money in the beginning than to see your pet being sad and lonely in the shelter. You should make sure that you understand this before you finalize on a cage for the pet.

A simple way to keep the Madagascar hissing cockroach happy is to give him an old t-shirt or piece of cloth. The Madagascar hissing cockroach will love it. He will act as if he is digging in the t-shirt. He will also try to fit in the t-shirt.

This will keep him busy and happy. This is will be one of his favourite playtimes. While the Madagascar hissing cockroach enjoys the old cloth, you can bask in the happiness of your beloved pet.

If you go to a Madagascar hissing cockroach toy shop, you will get many ideas for the accessories that you can keep in the cage of the pet. There are many types of bedding available these days that can help your Madagascar hissing cockroach to have rest and also fun when he wants.

You also have to make sure that the Madagascar hissing cockroach is entertained even at times when you are not around. The Madagascar hissing cockroach can get bored easily, which will make him a little aggressive. To keep him occupied, you can keep various kinds of toys in the Madagascar hissing cockroach's cage.

The right kind of toys should be bought for the Madagascar hissing cockroach. You will get many ideas when you visit a shop that keeps toys for Madagascar hissing cockroaches. But, it is important that the toys are made of a good quality. They should not be harmful for the pet. Your Madagascar hissing cockroach will take them in his mouth, so they should be of a good quality.

It is better if the toys are washable. This will enable you to wash the Madagascar hissing cockroach's toys every now and then when they are dirty. The harmful bacteria will also be removed from the toys when they are washed.

Also, make sure that the toys can't be shredded by the Madagascar hissing cockroach. If the pet is able to shred the toy, he will swallow the shreds. This is very harmful and will only invite more trouble for the pet. To avoid all these issues, buy the right kind of toys.

If you are planning to domesticate more than one Madagascar hissing cockroach, you can consider buying another cage. This cage could be very simple and basic. The main purpose of this extra cage is to use it when one of the Madagascar hissing cockroaches is sick. The cage will help you to isolate the sick Madagascar hissing cockroach.

A vet will always advise you to isolate a sick pet. This is necessary so that the pet can recuperate nicely in absence of other pets. He would need some space to himself. What is also important is that he should not transmit the disease to the healthy pets. The isolation helps to avoid such a situation also.

3. Cleaning the enclosure

Like it is important to clean the house that you dwell in, it is extremely important to clean the cage of the pet. You will not necessarily enjoy this process, but still you have to do it. The pet can't clean the cage on its own, and if it is forced to stay in an unhygienic environment, he will fall sick.

There are certain tasks that you need to do daily, while several others need to be done once a week. If the bedding is soiled, it should be cleaned on a daily basis. Similarly, if the food and water containers look dirty, they should be cleaned and refilled. The litter box needs to be cleared every day.

Once a week, you should clean the entire cage. You should thoroughly clean it with a clean cloth. Remember that the Madagascar hissing cockroach should not be in the cage when the cleaning procedure is going on. The litter box needs to be disinfected once a week. The toys of the Madagascar hissing cockroach should be washed once every two weeks, if the toys are washable.

The litter box and the floor of the cage can be cleaned with the help of a mixture of bleach and water. The mixture should have 98 per cent water and only two per cent bleach. This daily and weekly cleaning procedure is important so that the surroundings of the Madagascar hissing cockroach remain healthy. The bacteria in the dust and dirt can harm the Madagascar hissing cockroach.

While you are busy cleaning the cage of the pet Madagascar hissing cockroach, it is important that you check the cage thoroughly. If the Madagascar hissing cockroach has littered in an area other than the litter box, then it should be cleared and disinfected properly. You should make it a point to do this check on a daily basis.

You can keep baby wipes handy to clean something immediately. It is important that the cage is free from all bacteria and viruses that are known to cause diseases in pet animals. You should keep some time designated for the cleaning of the cage.

If you are using bleach to clean the litter box, then you should make sure that there are no residues on the box. The Madagascar hissing cockroach can try to lick on any residue that he may find on the box or the cage. Bleach can be very harmful and dangerous to the pet animal.

Another point that you need to understand is that you should not use very strong disinfectants. Such products can be very harmful if they ingested even in the smallest of quantities. You should always look for mild anti-bacterial soaps and detergents to clean the cage.

A simple procedure that you can follow once every week to clean the cage thoroughly is to fill a bucket with clean water. Pour some anti-bacterial detergent that you wish to use. Form a nice lather in the bucket. This can be used to clean the toys and the containers. The remaining can be used to clean the floor nicely.

After you have cleaned the floor with the detergent, use plain water to wash off any sign of the detergent. This will ensure that the Madagascar hissing cockroach does not ingest anything harmful.

It is also very important that you let the floor dry completely before you allow the Madagascar hissing cockroach to come inside the cage. He could spoil the floor and could create a mess for you to clean again. He could even try to drink any residue that he finds on the floor. To avoid all these hassles, you should allow the floor to dry completely.

Chapter 5: Cockroach proofing the house

When you have a Madagascar hissing cockroach at home, you have to ensure that the pet is safe at all times. The Madagascar hissing cockroach is so tiny that you might not know where he is most of times. This makes it very important that you understand the behaviour of your pet very well.

A Madagascar hissing cockroach has a very curious personality. He will not think twice before charging into unknown territory. You might be busy with some work, and before you know it, your pet Madagascar hissing cockroach might be walking into some real danger.

You should know that a Madagascar hissing cockroach has a tendency to injure himself. If you don't pay attention, the damage could be very serious and irrevocable. A solution to keep your Madagascar hissing cockroach safe is to cockroach proof your home. This chapter will discuss the potential dangers to the Madagascar hissing cockroaches and also some simple ways to Madagascar hissing cockroach proof your house.

1. How to cockroach proof the house?

This section will help you to understand the various ways to cockroach proof your home. Make sure you Madagascar hissing cockroach proof your home and keep your pet Madagascar hissing cockroach away from potential dangers. There is no use crying after the damage has been done. It is always better to take the necessary precautions in the very beginning.

To begin with, you should make sure that all liquid chemicals are far away from the Madagascar hissing cockroach. If a chemical is in reach of the Madagascar hissing cockroach, he might accidently spill it all over him. To make sure that nothing of the sort happens, you should make sure that all such supplies are kept in top cabinets where a Madagascar hissing cockroach can't reach.

You should also make sure that all kind of medicines, syrups and tablets are out of the reach of the Madagascar hissing cockroach. These can be very harmful for the pet. You can also get childproof cabinets in your home to keep all such potentially dangerous stuff in those cabinets.

You would be surprised to know that your pet can climb toilets. Just imagine what can happen if the seat is not kept down. The Madagascar hissing cockroach can slip inside and can get himself killed. To avert any such incident, make sure that he toilet seat is kept down. This should be especially done when the Madagascar hissing cockroach is around the toilet area.

You can also keep the toilet door closed to make sure that he does not enter the toilet. If there are any areas of the house that the Madagascar hissing cockroach needs to keep away from, you have to keep them closed and blocked. If you don't do so, the pet can just enter the space when you are not around.

You should make sure that the Madagascar hissing cockroach sleeps in his cage. This is for his safety and also for the good of the family members. You can also keep him in the cage when you can't supervise him and his actions.

You should make sure that your Madagascar hissing cockroach plays with the right kind of toys. Cheap plastic materials that can have an adverse effect on the health of the Madagascar hissing cockroach must be avoided. Similarly, toys that can be shredded or broken should also be avoided.

The Madagascar hissing cockroach might accidentally swallow the small or shredded pieces. Make sure that the toys that you allow the pet to play with are of good quality. They should be safe for the Madagascar hissing cockroach, and they should be impossible to swallow for the Madagascar hissing cockroach.

Your Madagascar hissing cockroach could actually shock you with the kind of things it can get hurt from.

You should make sure any such potentially dangerous things are out of the reach of the Madagascar hissing cockroach. Keep the waste bin and waste stuff away from him because he might try to play with things that could be harmful for him. This might be very difficult for you in the beginning to look into areas and places that have hidden dangers for the pet.

But, you will definitely learn with time and experience. The furniture in the house should be Madagascar hissing cockroach-friendly. You should make sure there are no sharp edges that could hurt the animal. Also, make sure that the Madagascar hissing cockroach can climb on the furniture.

If you have recliners in your house, keep them away from the pet. The pet could be severely injured by these reclining chairs. If somebody sits on them accidentally while the Madagascar hissing cockroach is hiding in the spring, the reclining action and the spring could injure the pet. To be on the safer side, always check the chair or sofa that you are about to sit on. You don't want to sit on your Madagascar hissing cockroach and injure him.

Your Madagascar hissing cockroach could climb into the washing machine and dish washer. So, make sure that these items always have a lid on. To be on the safer side, always check inside the washing machine and the dish washer before operating them.

The pet Madagascar hissing cockroach should stay away from the plants of the house. You should also make sure that he stays away from Styrofoam products. All kinds of sponges should not be in the reach of the Madagascar hissing cockroach. The Madagascar hissing cockroach could bite into them and swallow them. This can be potentially very dangerous.

Rubber items can also be very dangerous if they are swallowed by the pet Madagascar hissing cockroach. You should know that the Madagascar hissing cockroach will not know what he is not supposed to do. You will have to keep him away from danger.

Keep away all rubber products so that the pet can't reach them. This includes both soft rubber and foam rubber products. You should also make sure that soaps and detergents are kept away from the reach of the pet. These items can be very dangerous for the pet.

It is better to use the cabinets of bathrooms and rooms to keep things away from the pet Madagascar hissing cockroach. You should make sure that the pet stays away from stacks of clothes. Keep the cupboards locked and keep the laundry area closed and locked. If the Madagascar hissing cockroach gets inside a stack of clothes, you will have a very hard time finding him.

There could be so many things in your house that look non-dangerous, but could be very dangerous for your Madagascar hissing cockroach. This is the reason that you might have to monitor the pet animal when he is not in his cage.

It is also a good idea to designate a spare room in the house for the Madagascar hissing cockroach. This room should be open and spacious. It should have natural light and dim artificial lights. You can leave the Madagascar hissing cockroach in the room and be sure that he is playing and having a good time. Of course, this will totally depend on whether you can spare a room in the house or not.

2. Areas of hidden dangers

While a Madagascar hissing cockroach is a loveable and adorable pet, it can also be very destructive. As the owner, it is your responsibility to avoid any potential danger that the Madagascar hissing cockroach can do. If a Madagascar hissing cockroach is forced to stay in a cage for longer durations, he will get agitated and depressed.

You should allow the Madagascar hissing cockroach to feel free in your home. But, to be able to do so, you will have to Madagascar hissing cockroach proof your house. This means to create an environment where the Madagascar hissing cockroach is happy and minimum damage is done to the things in the house.

Creating such an environment is essential to the Madagascar hissing cockroach and also to the other family members. If you wish to make your home suitable for the Madagascar hissing cockroach then you should be ready to let off certain things.

You should not keep expensive carpets in areas where the pet will play because the Madagascar hissing cockroach will spoil it. Instead, make use of old rags and carpets.

Don't keep breakable pieces in reach of the Madagascar hissing cockroach. The Madagascar hissing cockroach will approach it and might destroy it or hurt himself. You should also not keep breakable things in reach of the pet Madagascar hissing cockroach.

There are certain food items that are very dangerous for the Madagascar hissing cockroach. You should make sure that the pet has no access to these items. Also, make sure that all chemicals and harmful substances are not reachable to him.

All the electrical equipment should be kept at a safe distance from the Madagascar hissing cockroach. The sockets should be covered so that the pet animal is not harmed. You should not leave any food items on the table or shelves. He might eat it, without knowing whether it is good for him or bad for him.

The washroom door should always be kept closed, especially the toilet seat. Make it a rule in the house to always keep the seat down. This will make it easier for you manage everything.

There should be no wires on the floor of the house. The Madagascar hissing cockroach can get entangled in these and can severely hurt himself. You should also keep all the doors and windows closed to not give him a chance to escape.

You should be very serious about Madagascar hissing cockroach proofing your home. It is known that gastro intestinal disorders can cause a Madagascar hissing cockroach to die very early in his life. Your Madagascar hissing cockroach could just chew something dangerous and die.

If your pet Madagascar hissing cockroach swallows something toxic for him, you might not even get a chance to take him to the veterinarian and save him.

The digestive system of the animal is such that blockages can happen easily and they can be very dangerous. There are many Madagascar hissing cockroaches that lose their lives because of such blockages.

This makes it very important to look for areas of hidden dangers and keep the pet safe. The Madagascar hissing cockroach will try to chew anything it can. It will chew on rubber items, though such things are very harmful for him. It is you who needs to make sure that the pet does not chew on the wrong items.

Madagascar hissing cockroaches are fond of chewing on rubber items and foam and sponge based products. While they might like chewing on them, these materials when ingested will cause blockage of the digestive tract. You have to take measures to avoid such incidents in your home.

Your pet will love the stuffing of your sofa and couch. He will try to climb on the furniture and try to chew on the stuffing. He will also not miss an opportunity to chew on paper, cardboard and plastic items. These things are extremely dangerous for him if he swallows them.

If you don't keep an eye out, your Madagascar hissing cockroach will chew away all your expensive sofas. Additionally, they like digging and tunnelling. So, the animal would try to dig in the sofa material.

You should be on the lookout of any tell-tale signs. If you see stuffing material on the floor, you should know what the Madagascar hissing cockroach has been up to. He should be stopped as soon as possible.

Keep away your shoes in a cupboard or cabinet. Before you know, your Madagascar hissing cockroach might start hiding in them and chewing on them.

You should also check the bedding of the pet on a regular basis. If he has been chewing on it, then you should try a better and stronger fabric. These things are very harmful for the Madagascar hissing cockroach.

Madagascar hissing cockroaches are also attracted to plants. They will merrily chew on the leaves of various plants. Many plants are known to be poisonous for the Madagascar hissing cockroach, so they should not be encouraged to eat the leaves.

The best thing to do will obviously be to keep the plats in an area where the Madagascar hissing cockroach can't reach them. This is a fool proof way to keep them away from the plants.

If you observe the pet closely, you will start understanding his likes and preferences. After you have kept an eye on him for a few days, you will start understanding his favourite spots in the house.

You will know which areas he likes to dig and where he prefers to hide. These pieces of information can help you to Madagascar hissing cockroach proof your home in a better way.

Your Madagascar hissing cockroach will be very attracted to the soaps and detergents. You need to be cautious when you are using store bought detergents and bleaching powder to clean surfaces and washrooms. A slight trace of the bleaching agent can be harmful for the pet.

The Madagascar hissing cockroach will go to a recently cleaned bath tub or toilet and lick the water off the surface. While this could be fun to watch for you, it could be dangerous if the tub and toilet still have traces of the detergent. To be on the safer side, you should always rinse the surfaces with excess water. This will make sure that the detergent has been washed off.

A Madagascar hissing cockroach has a tendency to walk in to a situation and then not know what to do next. He might just climb on to the top of a closet, not knowing what to do.

Madagascar hissing cockroaches will also crawl into any opening they see. For example, a Madagascar hissing cockroach might get under the small opening of a fridge or refrigerator. This is very dangerous because the fan of the fridge can harm him.

Similarly, washing machines and dish washers are potential dangers to the animal. The best way to keep your pet animal out of danger is to know where he is and what he is up to. This will mean that you can help him if he has landed himself into some kind of danger.

You might also have to use barriers to make sure that the Madagascar hissing cockroach can't reach certain spots and rooms in the house. But, a point that needs to be noted here is that normal pet barriers can't be used for a Madagascar hissing cockroach.

Even child proofing barriers would not be effective. This is because your Madagascar hissing cockroach will happily climb these barriers.

You will have to make safe and secure barriers on your own. Or, you could get these barriers from a Madagascar hissing cockroach shop.

These barriers have a very strong base of plastic. Barriers made of Plexiglas will also serve the purpose right. If you wish to make the barrier at your home, then you can use Plexiglas or wood.

You can also use a good piece of cardboard as a barrier. For example, to keep the Madagascar hissing cockroach away from the fridge or refrigerator, you can fix the cardboard in the opening. This will prevent the pet from entering the opening. Make sure you use a good quality cardboard.

You can also take some measures to keep the Madagascar hissing cockroach away from your furniture. This is important so that they don't try to create a tunnel by chewing on the fabric. You can fix some heavy material of cardboard at the bottom end of the furniture that you are trying to protect.

This can prevent the pet from digging on the material of the furniture. You can also keep such barriers in front of various rooms. This will make sure that the pet can't enter these rooms. These are simple ways to keep the pet safe and also your things safe.

It is important that you take appropriate steps to Madagascar hissing cockroach proof the home. This will help you to set some limits and boundaries for the pet. These boundaries are for his own good.

There is no use in getting cautious after serious and irrevocable damage has been done. It pays to take all the necessary precautions right from the very beginning.

You will take some time to understand the mannerisms of your pet. It is important to always supervise the pet. If you are unable to do so, you can ask a family member to do so for you. You can use the cage when there is no one around to supervise the pet Madagascar hissing cockroach.

You can be secure knowing that your pet is safe and sound inside its cage. But, once you understand the pet better, you can take further steps to make sure that things remain safe in the house for the pet. A safe environment is good for everybody in the home.

Chapter 6: Diet requirements of the Madagascar hissing cockroach

As the owner or as the prospective owner of a Madagascar hissing cockroach, it should be your foremost concern to provide adequate and proper nutrition to the pet. If the pet animal is deficient in any nutrient, he will develop various deficiencies and acquire many diseases. When the nutrition is right, you can easily ward off many dangerous diseases.

The staple diet of an animal depends on its natural habitat and the food available around the habitat. Madagascar hissing cockroaches are known to feed on available food in their natural habitat. This is their staple diet.

When you domesticate an animal you can't keep it devoid of its natural and staple food. The digestive tract of the animal is also tuned to digest the staple food. You should always keep these points in mind.

Each animal species is different. Just because certain kinds of foods are good for your pet dog, it does not mean that they will be good for your pet Madagascar hissing cockroach also. It is important to learn about all the foods that the Madagascar hissing cockroaches are naturally inclined towards eating. You should always be looking at maintaining good health of your pet.

It is important to learn about the foods that are good for your Madagascar hissing cockroach. But, you should also understand that the foods that you feed your pet with could be lacking in certain nutrients. An animal in the wild is different from one in captivity. Availability of certain foods will also affect the diet of your pet.

Generally, the food given to captive pets is lacking in certain nutrients. It is not able to provide the pet with all the necessary nutrients. If such a case, you will have to give commercial pellets to your Madagascar hissing cockroach. These pellets are known to compensate for the various nutritional deficiencies that the animal might have due to malnutrition.

You should always aim at providing wholesome nutrition to your pet. It is important to understand the pet's nutritional requirements and include all the nutrients in his daily meals. To meet his nutritional requirements, you might also have to give him certain supplements.

The supplements will help you to make up for the essential nutrients that are not found in his daily meals. Though these supplements are easily available, you should definitely consult a veterinarian before you give your Madagascar hissing cockroach any kind of supplements.

It is very important that you serve only high quality food to your pet. If you are trying to save some money by buying cheaper low quality alternatives, then you are in a bad situation. Low quality food will affect the health of the Madagascar hissing cockroach.

You can expect him to acquire deficiencies and diseases when he is not fed good quality food. The cure for this is taking the pet to the veterinarian. This in turn will only cost you more money.

To avoid this endless loop, it is better to work on the basics. Keep the pet healthy by feeding him with high quality foods, rather than spending money on him by taking him to the veterinarian.

1. What does the Madagascar hissing cockroach eat in the wild?

When you are looking to plan the food for your pet roach, it will serve you to understand what the pet animal eats in the wild. The Madagascar hissing cockroach is an opportunistic feeder. This means that the hissing cockroach will tweak its preferences to what is available. The insect will survive on what it finds to eat.

In its natural habitat, the insect feeds on fruits that have fallen off the tress. The fruits in the rainforest help the insect to derive the moisture that it needs to survive. In captivity, you can experiment with more foods because the cockroach is capable of digesting a wide variety of foods as long as it is getting the right water content.

Moisture levels

A roach needs good amounts of water in its diet. It is capable of digesting a wide variety of foods as long as it is getting the right water content.

In the wild, the roach drinks dew drops from the leaves, vegetables and fruits. You should make sure that the roach gets adequate moisture in the diet, which can be done by giving good amounts of water.

Dry foods

A roach can easily survive on dried foods. You can feed your roach on cat food and fish pellets. Certain kinds of dog foods will also be fine. The key is to make sure that they get adequate moisture in the diet, which can be done by giving good amounts of water.

Vegetables and fruits

In its natural habitat, the insect feeds on fruits and vegetables that have fallen off the tress. The fruits and the vegetables in the rain forest help the insect to derive the moisture that it needs to survive.

You can also serve fruits and vegetables as the main food items to your pet cockroach. There is a wide range of the fruits and vegetables that you can serve the pet insect.

Serving vegetables and fruits is also easier as they are available all year round. The various vegetables and fruits that can be served to the insect are sweet potatoes, banana, orange slices, grapes, apples, carrots and potato slices.

It is important that foods with high moisture are served in small slices of about inch. This prevents formation of fermentation gases which will be detrimental for the cockroach.

2. Nutritional needs

The food that you give to your Madagascar hissing cockroach should be capable of meeting its entire nutritional requirements. The food should appeal to the pet in terms of taste. He should want to eat it, and at the same time it should also provide the pet with all the necessary nutrients.

Meeting the nutritional requirements of the pet can be the biggest concern while looking to domesticate a pet Madagascar hissing cockroach. You have to make sure that you understand the diet requirements of the Madagascar hissing cockroach before you can decide to domesticate it.

It is critical that you understand the specific nutritional needs of your pet Madagascar hissing cockroach. A Madagascar hissing cockroach that dwells freely in the wild is used to having a high protein diet. This protein basically comes from the carnivorous diet of the Madagascar hissing cockroach.

Madagascar hissing cockroaches love food with moisture. If you are planning to keep your Madagascar hissing cockroach on a strict plant diet, then you can do so easily.

These animals need moisture and protein in their diet. The food that you serve to the Madagascar hissing cockroach should have at least 35 per cent of protein. It is better if the amount of protein is more than 35 per cent.

The food of a Madagascar hissing cockroach should also be rich in fats. The diet of the Madagascar hissing cockroach in the wild provides it with all the necessary fats. The fat content should be at least 20 per cent of the food. The protein and the fat in the diet of the Madagascar hissing cockroach are suited to the kind of digestive system that it has.

The digestive tract of a Madagascar hissing cockroach is quite small. This kind of digestive tract is suitable to digest good quality and easy to digest animal protein. It is not very suitable for food items such as corn, grain, and large quantities of vegetables and fruits. The main component of your Madagascar hissing cockroach's main feed should be protein.

The Madagascar hissing cockroach also needs the nutrient taurine. This is utilized for the cardiovascular system of the Madagascar hissing cockroach and also for the eyes. The food that you serve your pet should have sufficient quantities of taurine. This means that you should keep the pet away from dog food because it is known to lack in this vital nutrient.

Also, the Madagascar hissing cockroach needs more animal protein for maintaining its body functions. Dog food is known to be rich in plant protein, but not animal protein. Cecum is a part of the digestive system that helps the body to break down plant proteins. Madagascar hissing cockroaches don't have Cecum in their body.

3. Every day diet of the Madagascar hissing cockroaches

If you are looking at buying food from the grocery store, then don't forget to check all the ingredients. If the main component is not meat, then you should leave the food item. There will be many food items that will have cereal or corn or grain as the main ingredient. You should avoid such food items.

You should look for Madagascar hissing cockroach foods in the pet shop to get the best food for your pet. Cat food or kitten food will not be the best buy for your pet. These food items will be unable to provide the right kind of nutrition to the Madagascar hissing cockroach.

In case Madagascar hissing cockroach food is not available in your area and you are only left with the choice of kitten and cat food, then you should consult a veterinarian for the right cat food. There are all sorts of cat foods available. You should buy the one that is the best for your Madagascar hissing cockroach. Even in this case, you have to use fatty acid supplements along with the food to make up for the lack of fatty acids in cat and kitten food.

It is always a good idea to consult a vet in case of any doubts that you might be having regarding the diet and foods of the Madagascar hissing cockroach. One of the best food items that takes care of the protein and the fat content required by the Madagascar hissing cockroach is cat food. It has over 35 per cent protein and over 20 per cent fat that are essential for the growth of the Madagascar hissing cockroach.

The main component of the Madagascar hissing cockroach's meal should be chicken. You can replace chicken with lamb if you wish to. If you are looking for Madagascar hissing cockroach foods, then this should be the main ingredient of the food item. Don't forget to check the percentage of each nutrient in the food item.

Many a times, store bought foods are preserved by artificial means. You should not be buying such food products for your Madagascar hissing cockroach. If the food item is preserved with the addition of Vitamin E in it, then this food is healthy for your Madagascar hissing cockroach. It is also important that the food item is not loaded with artificial colours.

As the parent of the pet Madagascar hissing cockroach, you will be required to make smart choices in order to provide wholesome nutrition to your pet. Another thing that you need to make sure while buying food for Madagascar hissing cockroach is that the food should not have vegetables and fruits in dry form. This is extremely unhealthy for the pet.

Dried forms of vegetables and fruits are easily available; so many manufacturers might decide to use them. But, they can cause a serious health hazard to your pet Madagascar hissing cockroach. They can get stuck in the digestive tract or intestine and can cause very harmful gastro-intestinal issues. You should also avoid any food that has a high percentage of corn or grain or both.

You should make sure that your Madagascar hissing cockroach is getting optimal nutrition in his diet. His food should provide him with all the essential nutrients and vitamins. A high quality Madagascar hissing cockroach food will help you to fulfil the daily nutritional requirements of the Madagascar hissing cockroach. These foods will contain animal protein and all other nutrients in the right quantity.

Over a period of time, the skin of the pet can start to dull. This is one of the first signals that something is not right with the pet's health. The malnutrition will result in many other health issues. In severe cases, you can also expect kidney stones to form along with bladder stones. The reason for these stones is the excess fibre in the cat and kitten food.

If you have no other choice but to choose from cat and kitten food, then you should definitely go for kitten food. The reason behind this choice is that kitten food has a relatively higher percentage of protein when compared with equal quantities of cat food. Also, the fat content of kitten food is much higher than similar quantities of cat food.

It is also important to note that if a larger quantity of cat food is fed to the Madagascar hissing cockroach for a longer duration of time, then the Madagascar hissing cockroach can be diagnosed with allergies. This is the reason that you need to consult the vet before feeding the pet with any other food apart from Madagascar hissing cockroach food.

In case you have been feeding the Madagascar hissing cockroach with the wrong kind of foods, you need to switch as soon as possible. No matter how much damage has been done, you can still avert a lot of damage. So, never fail to make the right choices and right switches.

Your food choices will be limited by the area where you live. But, there is always a way to make sure that the optimal thing is being done for the Madagascar hissing cockroach. There are many people who feed their pet

Madagascar hissing cockroach with cooked chicken along with standard kitten food. This makes sure that the Madagascar hissing cockroach gets optimal amounts of protein and fat.

Another alternative that you can consider to supplement the main meals of the pet Madagascar hissing cockroach is the easily available chick food. You should make sure that this is only a supplement and not the regular meal. While you allow your pet to chew and the lick the food, you should make sure that the food items are of the right size.

If the items are too small in size, the pet might just swallow the entire piece, leading to a detrimental blockage of the digestive tract. You should give bigger items that can only be licked but not swallowed. In case you wish to feed the Madagascar hissing cockroach with the vegetables, make sure you boil these before serving them to the pet. This will make the vegetables softer for the pet.

It is always better if you can feed the Madagascar hissing cockroach with high quality Madagascar hissing cockroach food and also raw vegetables and fruits with it. A diet like this will take care of nutritional requirement of the pet. The pet should have access to water and also food at all times. You need not worry about the Madagascar hissing cockroach over-eating. It is known that these animals don't overeat. They eat as much as is required by their body, but they need frequent meals so it better that they have easy access to food.

The pet would require almost 5-7 small meals in a day, owning to the fast metabolism of the Madagascar hissing cockroach. The water can be kept in a container with a heavy base. Also, keep some water in a water bottle that can hang from the cage. You should change the contents of the containers twice a day. You might have to do it more times if the pet has soiled the food or water while playing.

You may have to make changes to the Madagascar hissing cockroach's diet as it grows older. It is known that older Madagascar hissing cockroaches can have kidney issues. To lower the pressure on the kidneys, you should give the pet a diet low in animal protein.

4. Water wick vs water dish

Just because your cockroach is very tiny does not mean that it will not require good quantities of water. You will have to provide good supplies of water in the tank of the roach.

There are a few concerns that a new pet parent will have regarding keeping water in the tank of the cockroach.

How much water should I keep?

What if the cockroach drowns in the water kept in the tank?

These are very genuine concerns. This section will help you to clear all these issues.

It is true that if the water dish has too much water, it can cause more harm to the roach than good. The cockroach can drown in the water dish. So, it is important that you keep the right amount of water for the insect.

You can keep a water dish in the tank of the insect. Remember to fill the water dish only up to the right level. The water level should be shallow.

You can leave a sponge or a cotton wool in the water dish. This simple trick will make sure that the cockroach does not drown in the water dish even if it accidentally slips in.

You need to understand here that no matter what precautions you take, there is a possibility that your tiny insect can drown in the water dish. To avoid any such mishap you need to keep a constant eye on the pet insect.

There is another option to keep water in the tank of the roach. This option is considered a better buy than keeping the water filled water dish in the tank of the roach.

There are many pet shops that will make these water wicks for you. You can look around for them. You can also order them online. You can also make them at home. They are actually very easy to make at home.

Take a very small container. This container should have a lid. Now drill a hole in this lid of the container. Make sure that the hole is very small otherwise all the water will just drain out.

You should take a wick that will fit in the hole in the container nicely. This wick can be a string or can be cotton wool. You can use whatever is available. Fill some water in the small container and arrange the wick properly.

The cockroach will use the wick to drink the water. The water wick made of cotton wool or wool string will naturally absorb water which the roach will drink.

This simple method will eliminate the risk of the roach slipping in the water dish and drowning.

5. Treats

Treats are an essential part of a pet's meal plan. Treats are like small meal gifts that make the pet happy and delighted. The anticipation of getting a treat can also keep his behaviour in check.

You should work on giving your pet high quality treats. The treat should be tasty and also nutritious. The Madagascar hissing cockroach should look forward to receiving a treat from you. This section will give you an idea of the kind of treats you can include in your Madagascar hissing cockroach's meal plan.

It should be noted that just because your Madagascar hissing cockroach seems to enjoy a treat, you can't give the food item to him all day long. You will have to keep a check on the amount of treats a Madagascar hissing cockroach will get. This is important because treats are not food replacements. They are only small rewards.

It is also important that the pet Madagascar hissing cockroach associates the treat with reward. He should know that he is being served the treat reward for a reason. You should also make sure that the treats are healthy for the pet.

If you keep serving him the wrong kinds of treats, it will only affect his health in the long run. This is the last thing that you would want as a parent of the pet.

This section will help you to understand various kinds of treats that you can serve your pet. The best kind of treat for a Madagascar hissing cockroach is a food item that has meat as its main component. Madagascar hissing cockroaches love their meat, and it is also healthy for them.

You should always look for treats that are healthy for the pet. The pet should enjoy eating them, but their nutrition should not be compromised. Your main aim should be to satisfy the pet's taste buds and also provide him some nutrition.

You should also make an attempt to understand what is there in the treat that you prefer for the Madagascar hissing cockroach. If you know the contents and their exact quantities, it will only get easier for you to make a well informed decision. Various pet shops will have Madagascar hissing cockroach foods that will help you to make a decision regarding the pet's treats.

The treat should have the right mix of vitamins, fatty acids, minerals and proteins. This will make the treat healthy and wholesome. It is better if the treat has no sugar content.

This is because the sugar will add no food value to the treat. Such healthy treats can be given to the pet Madagascar hissing cockroach on a daily basis without any issues.

Be careful if you are planning to give your pet a bowl of fruits as a treat. If you think that any fruit or vegetable can serve as a treat for the pet, then you are absolutely wrong.

The pet can suffer from diarrhoea and other gastro intestinal-problems. It is important to give the right kind of fruits. The pet can be safely given apples and bananas.

You will be shocked to know the problems that an undigested vegetables or fruits can cause in a Madagascar hissing cockroach.

If there is a piece of undigested fruit or vegetable in the digestive tract of the animal, it can lead to obstructions and blockages. This will lead to many other digestive tract related complications.

The bowel movements of the pet can be restricted or completely stopped because of the undigested food. This can even pose a very serious threat to the life of the animal.

Also, you should make sure that you peel and mash the items before you serve them to the animal. This will allow him to digest the food well. There have been many reports of blockages in Madagascar hissing cockroaches because of undigested carrots.

If you serve an uncooked carrot to the Madagascar hissing cockroach, there is a very high chance that the Madagascar hissing cockroach will be unable to digest it, leading to a urinary blockage.

You can also give him a small piece of kibble. Remember to keep the quantity very low because this can increase the sugar content in the pet's body and can also lead to toxicity.

You should keep in mind that you shouldn't serve something as a treat to the pet just because you like the food item. The food item should not harm the very sensitive digestive tract of the Madagascar hissing cockroach.

As a rule, stay away from sodas, dairy products that are not for lactose intolerance, candy bars, chocolate pieces, caffeine, nuts and excessively salty and sugary foods.

These food items can cause some serious damage to the Madagascar hissing cockroach. For example, if a nut gets stuck in the digestive tract, it can even kill the Madagascar hissing cockroach. Excessive amounts of sugar can directly affect the work of the pancreas and the blood sugar level in the body.

Dairy products are known to cause gastro-intestinal issues in these animals. Also, a large amount of salt is unhealthy for the Madagascar hissing cockroach. He can get really sick if you feed him with foods such as chips.

Look for Madagascar hissing cockroach foods or kitten foods that can be served as treats. For example, kitten food is a great example of a nutritious yet tasty treat for the Madagascar hissing cockroach. Another example of a great treat is Gerber baby food.

Give your pet different kinds of Madagascar hissing cockroach foods so that you get a lot of options to choose from. You can also buy small chew toys for him from the Madagascar hissing cockroach store.

The Madagascar hissing cockroach will love this. You can also give him shreds of cooked vegetables or small pieces of cooked carrots or potatoes.

6. Supplements

The diet of the Madagascar hissing cockroach should be highly nutritious. If you make sure that the Madagascar hissing cockroach is getting all its necessary nutrients from the food itself, you can avoid the use of supplements.

At times, your Madagascar hissing cockroach's diet might not be able to provide it with the right set of nutrients and vitamins. In such a case, it becomes necessary to introduce supplements in the diet of the Madagascar hissing cockroach.

If the pet is not well and is recuperating from an injury or disease, the veterinarian might advise you to administer certain supplements to the pet. These supplements will help the pet to heal faster and get back on his feet sooner.

You should always consult a veterinarian before you administer any supplement to the Madagascar hissing cockroach. He will be the best judge of which supplements the Madagascar hissing cockroach requires and which ones he doesn't.

There are many vitamin supplements that are available in tasty treat forms for the Madagascar hissing cockroach. While you can be sure that your pet is getting the right nutrients, the pet can enjoy the treat given to him.

You can also include supplements of fatty acids in the diet of the Madagascar hissing cockroach. A few drops of this kind of supplement will enhance the taste and the nutritional value of the food item that is being served to the Madagascar hissing cockroach.

While it can be necessary to supplement certain vitamins and nutrients to the pet, you should also be aware of the hazards of over-feeding a certain nutrient. If there is an overdose of a certain vitamin in the body of the Madagascar hissing cockroach, it can lead to vitamin toxicity.

Vitamin toxicity is very common in Madagascar hissing cockroaches. You should try to feed the Madagascar hissing cockroach with an optimal amount of Vitamins to avoid such a condition.

You might even see that your pet is enjoying all the supplements, but this in no way means that you can give him an overdose. You should always do what is right for the Madagascar hissing cockroach's health.

Another point that you should take care of is that you should not blindly follow the instructions and dosage that is printed on various supplements. The food that you feed the Madagascar hissing cockroach will also have a supply of vitamins. The Madagascar hissing cockroach will only require some extra dosage.

On a regular basis, you can look at giving the Madagascar hissing cockroach treats with supplements. These can be given on a daily basis, but the portions need to be controlled.

You can add 3-6 drops or pea-sized portion of supplements. This is enough to supplement the daily requirements of the Madagascar hissing cockroach.

Chapter 7: Health of the Madagascar hissing cockroach

An unhealthy pet can be a nightmare for any owner. The last thing that you would want is to see your pet lying down in pain. Many disease causing parasites dwell in unhygienic places and food. If you take care of the hygiene and food of the Madagascar hissing cockroach, there are many diseases that you can avert.

You should make sure that you do your best to prevent diseases by taking all the necessary precautions. If proper care is given to the food served to the pet, many diseases can be avoided.

You should always make sure that your pet Madagascar hissing cockroach is always kept in a clean environment. A neat and clean environment will help you to keep off many common ailments and diseases.

You should make sure that the Madagascar hissing cockroach has all his vaccines on time. Apart from this, you should take him for regular check-ups to the veterinarian. This is important so that even the smallest health issue can be tracked at an early stage.

At times, even after all the precautions that you take, the pet can get sick. It is always better to be well equipped so that you can help your pet. You should always consult a vet when you find any unusual traits and symptoms in the pet.

You should understand the various health related issues that your pet Madagascar hissing cockroach can suffer from. This knowledge will help you to get the right treatment at the right time. It is also important that you understand how you can take care of a sick pet. This knowledge will help you to keep calm and help the sick Madagascar hissing cockroach.

1. When should you see the veterinarian?

If you find your pet behaving different from normal, then the first step you should take is to provide him warmth. It is important that the pet is not cold and proper temperature is maintained.

Even after that if you see them deteriorating, it is time to see the veterinarian. If the condition is not very severe, you can book an appointment in the next three to four days.

But if there is an emergency, you should not waste time and should take the cockroach to the veterinarian as soon as possible. You can also take him to the emergency clinic in your locality.

It is important that you are able to identify the signs of emergency in your pet so that you can act without delay. If you happen to notice the following in your pet cockroach, you should know that it is an emergency and the veterinarian needs to be consulted:

- **Lethargy**: If the pet is not moving at all, try to increase the heat for him. If the pet remains to be unresponsive even after that, this can be serious. Don't do something drastic such as putting a stick in the water bed. Just take him to the doctor.

- **Diarrhoea**: If the problem of diarrhoea or green stools persists for more than two days, you will have to get the faecal exam done for any complications. After you have domesticated a cockroach for a while, you will be able to identify normal faeces and loose faeces.

- **Blood**: Blood from an arm or a small cut is not a thing to worry about. But, blood from urine or the mouth is a cause of serious concern. It can get critical if not treated on time.

- **Vomits**: You might be surprised to learn that cockroaches can vomit like many other animals. Any undigested food is immediately vomited. Vomit caused by poisoning, choking or sickness should not be ignored at any cost. You should be able to identify the vomit of the cockroach so that you can take action.

- If you see the pet gasping for breath, or if you notice twitching or abnormal movements of limbs, you should consult the veterinarian as soon as possible.

Though it is always advised to take the pet to the vet if any health problem arises, it is always a great idea to keep a first aid kit ready. This will help in case of minor injuries and also emergencies when you can't reach the vet.

The main aim of a first aid is to give the pet some relief from his pain. Giving first aid would not be very difficult if you follow the right steps in the right order.

While you are giving the animal some first aid, there are a few things that you should do. This will help you to calm the cockroach and also give him the necessary aid.

You should make sure that you don't aggravate the pain and misery of the poor animal in any way. You should follow the given procedures in the given order to help the cockroach.

You should make sure that the airway of the animal is not blocked. Make sure that the cockroach is able to breathe properly.

After you have made sure that the animal is breathing properly, it is important to check if he is bleeding. If the animal is bleeding, you should take the necessary steps to stop his bleeding.

You should also be able to examine how profusely he is bleeding. After you have succeeded in reducing the bleeding of the cockroach, you have to take the necessary steps to maintain the right temperature of the pet animal.

If the body temperature is not maintained, it will worsen the condition of the pet. You should understand that pet cockroach is easily prone to stress. Injury and pain are two factors that can stress him a lot.

So, it is important that you take the necessary steps to reduce his stress levels. This might seem like an impossible and daunting task, but if you take the right steps, you will be able to calm your animal successfully.

When you keep a first aid kit, it is important that you have knowledge about each item. You should know how to use things. You should also replace stuff when they reach their expiration date.

The various items that the first aid box of the cockroach should have are bottled water, hand warmers, paper towels, flash light, toilet paper, scissors, tweezers, cotton swabs, hydrogen peroxide, saline water, Neosporin and ensure.

When you are giving first aid to your pet, you should check their body temperature. They should neither be too hot or too cold. The roaches need to maintain a warm body temperature at all times. When they are stressed or injured, it is all the more important for them to maintain a warm body temperature.

Roaches have a lower body temperature when compared to the body temperature of the human beings. You should check the temperature of the animal. If he is hypothermic, you should make arrangements to keep him warm from the outside.

You should make sure that the pet is not overheated. Too much heat is not good for your pet. It can disrupt many normal functions of the cockroach. If the pet is overheated, make sure that you cool him down.

This step becomes all the more important when you are dealing with roaches. They will be unable to regulate their temperature. So, when you provide them with first aid, you will have to regulate their body temperature.

It is advised to maintain regular health records for your pet. This will help you to understand his health in a better way. You would be able to detect even the smallest of issues with the help of these records.

For example, if you have a record of his size, you can notice any changes in the pet's weight. A drastic change in weight is often understood as an early symptom for diseases.

The pet can be saved from future health issues by keeping a simple record. If you can't keep a daily record, aim at a weekly record. Record all the important parameters at the beginning of each week and compare with the previous week.

The parameters that you should be aiming to record are the weight of the pet, the physical activity of the pet and the food intake of the pet.

You can calculate the quantity of food that the pet consumes by weighing the food that you serve and then the food that is left.

You can record the physical activity by observing and estimating the time. You should also look out for any gunk formation or lump formation on the body of the pet. You should also make sure that there are no trappings of hair around the limbs of the pet.

A lethargic pet that shows no interest in movement is not a good sign. You will only know these things if you observe. If you notice any change in the pet's normal activity levels or weight, you should be alerted.

This definitely means that something is wrong with the pet. An early action can save you from many health problems in the pet. This is good both for you and the pet.

2. Examining injuries in the cockroach

Cockroaches, like the other invertebrates, lead a very active lifestyle. They like moving around. Your pet is likely to spend most of its time doing so. This makes it susceptible to injuries.

There is nothing to worry about if your pet injures itself. You should be able to diagnose the injuries so that they can be treated well. You might even have to call the doctor from the doctor's clinic.

It is important that you learn the basics of diagnosing the injuries. This is important because if a small injury is treated well, the animal can be saved from a major problem in the future.

It is important that you understand that your pet animal might not show any signs of injuries, even when it is injured. It will be your responsibility to diagnose the injury before it turns into a bigger problem.

Looking for the symptoms of injuries

You should be on the lookout for any symptoms that your cockroach might display when it is injured. These symptoms could mean that there is something wrong with your cockroach. You should look carefully for the following symptoms:

- Is your cockroach looking very disturbed? This could be because he is in pain.

- Is your pet looking very lazy and lethargic? This could be because he has injured himself and is in pain.

- The limbs of the animal could also be hanging. This is also a clear sign of injury to the pet. You should closely examine his limbs to be sure.

- Is your pet in a stumbling position? Is the pet showing uncoordinated movements?

- The pet could be having frequent or infrequent fits.

- If there is a change in the way he carries himself, then this could also mean that the injury has forced the pet to change the way he usually is.

- You should look out for the faeces of the animal. If there is any change in the colour of the faeces, this could mean that there is something wrong with his health.

- Do you spot any blood on the skin of the animal? You should look for blood stains in the enclosure of the animal also. This could mean that something is not right.

- Look for certain common symptoms, such as coughing and vomiting by the animal.

- Do you witness any changes in the skin of the pet? If yes, then this could also mean that there is something that needs your attention.

- If your pet looks scared and tensed, you should understand that it is for a reason. You need to closely examine him to find out what is wrong.

When you spot any of the given symptoms in your pet, you should know that something is not right. You will have to take a closer look at the pet and examine. This examination will help you to understand if there is something wrong with your pet.

While you are examining your pet, you should also understand that your pet could be scared. It is important that you make the pet feel comfortable. This will help you conduct the examination properly and without any problems.

To make sure that the pet animal is not terrified when you are trying to examine him for any potential injuries, you can do the following:

You should make sure that you conduct the examination in a closed area, a place where the animal feels safe and protected. You should try to examine him indoors.

Do not let the place be crowded when the examination is being conducted. Make sure that all the other pets and your family members are outside and not in the same place where the examination is being conducted.

The noise level around you should be as low as possible. The noise will stress the pet and will irritate him, so make sure there is no noise around. Conduct the examination in a quiet place.

Be as gentle and kind as possible. This will help your pet to relax and feel less stressed. You should in no way add to the stress and pain of the pet.

Make sure that all the tools that are needed for the examination are ready. You shouldn't leave your pet alone to fetch the tools. Everything should be ready before the examination.

You should check his entire body. Remember to check on both sides of the body. Start the examination at one particular point and then move ahead from that point. The examination should be definite and guided and not random.

Look at how your pet responds to the body examination being done. If you feel that the animal is not taking it too well, you should stop the examination. You should look for any stress signs that he displays. You should not ignore them; otherwise the animal can go into deep shock.

3. Stress in cockroaches

If the cockroach does not get proper heat and light, he can go into stress mode. His senses start to shut down. It should be noted that hibernation is not good for pet cockroaches.

When the surroundings get very cold for the pet and the daylight shortens, the cockroach's body starts reacting differently. This is not natural for them.

After years and years of captivity, the cockroaches have also changed. They are dependent on consistent warm temperature for their well-being. Their bodies are not suitable to bear extremely cold weather or extremely hot weather.

When there is a decrease in temperature or change in light cycles, the cockroach will panic. But, the body will give up very soon.

If too much time is lost, the cockroach will not be able to come out of the state. You can even lose your cockroach. As the owner of the cockroach, it is important that you make sure that your pet does not go into this state. If this happens, things can get very complicated.

Your primary focus should be that the cockroach remains healthy. This can be done by maintaining warm temperatures around the cockroach.

You should make sure that there is a light cycle that is consistently maintained in the water tank of the pet. The water should also be at a consistent warm temperature.

You should also make an attempt to understand the signs of stress. If you see your pet going into that zone, you can make temperature and light changes in his surroundings to bring him back to normal.

If you could touch the stomach area of the pet, it will be cold. The pet might also act very unusual. These are warning signals that the pet is getting stressed and shouldn't be ignored at all.

The first thing that you should do after encountering such warning signals is to warm the cockroach. You should not increase the temperature all of a sudden. Do it gradually and consistently.

If you increase the temperature all of a sudden, the pet might go into a shocked state. You can use a heater to warm the tank, but the heater will need a lot of regulation so that it does not get too hot.

If the pet does not respond for a very long time, it is advised that you call the veterinarian. The immune system of the pet will also suffer when he is trying to recuperate. Once you have brought him back, you should take extra care of him.

Make sure he is away from anything that can make him sick. You should keep an eye on the pet and lookout for signals.

A simpler way to avoid the pet getting stressed again is to keep the temperature of the tank a few degrees more than what is normal for the cockroach.

Signs of stress

There are a few symptoms that will help you to identify stress in your pet. You should stop the body examination as soon as you spot any of these symptoms. The following signs will help you to identify stress:

- The pet will try to escape you when it is stressed. It will not let you come closer to him and will get irritated.

- The pet will show violent movements.

- The animal will show a drastic change in its activity level. There are a few animals that will get extremely active, while others will become very lethargic. They will not move at all.

- The pet would be seen grinding its body parts tightly and also flicking them.

- He would make strange and loud noises.

- If you measure the body temperature of the animal, there will be a change.

- The cockroach can eat its own arms when it is in stress. This is a self-cannibalism. It is very common in many species of cockroaches.

- The animal would lick his various body parts, such as legs and feet.

- The young ones would show the symptom of diarrhoea. They will suffer from frequent and liquid stools.

- If the animal is not treated on time, you will see that his appetite decreases with time. It will decrease to a point that it will become difficult for the animal to carry on his daily tasks.

Reducing stress

At this juncture, you would want to reduce the amount of stress that your cockroach must be going through. It is important that you take all the necessary steps to make the cockroach feel safe and secure.

- If your pet is still very young, then you should keep his tank in a secure and closed area. This will fill him with warmth. This is like a reassurance to the animal that he can be safe and secure.

- You should make sure that your pet can rest well in a calm environment. Keep him away from any place of commotion.

- Make sure that there are no noises around the animal. Any kind of noise will disrupt him and will agitate him.

- You should also try your best to make sure that there are no sudden noises around the cockroach. The animal should be able to rest in a calm environment. Sudden noises and voices will disturb the pet and will agitate him further. It should be made certain that all the noises are eliminated.

4. Common health issues

Madagascar hissing cockroaches are prone to certain diseases such as adrenal diseases. You should know that the unique digestive system, fast metabolism and smaller size can cause the pet to get sick very easily. If proper care is not taken, you will find your pet getting sick very often.

This section will help you to understand the various diseases that a Madagascar hissing cockroach can suffer from. The various symptoms and causes are also discussed in detail. This will help you to recognize a symptom, which could have otherwise gone unnoticed.

Though the section helps you to understand the various common health problems of the Madagascar hissing cockroach, it should be understood that a vet should be consulted in case of any health related issues. A vet will physically examine the pet and suggest what is best for your pet Madagascar hissing cockroach.

The various diseases that your Madagascar hissing cockroach can suffer from are listed in this section.

Understanding various diseases and their symptoms

Who wouldn't want their pets to be healthy? Nobody would want to see a helpless animal suffering from a disease. To make sure that your cockroach enjoys good health at all times, it is important that you recognize the symptoms of diseases that can affect a cockroach at an early stage.

If you can detect a disease at an early stage, there are more chances that the disease will be cured. To be able to do so, you should make an attempt to understand the various diseases that can affect a cockroach along with their symptoms.

It is known that cockroaches are not susceptible to diseases if they are given a good diet and given a good and clean environment. But, it is also known that cockroaches are easily stressed.

They get insecure easily, which increases their stress. They are very sensitive to stress and you will have to make special efforts to keep the animal calm, safe and secure.

You should always make sure that your pet is always kept in a clean environment. A neat and clean environment will help you to keep off many common ailments and diseases.

There are some common health issues that your cockroach is prone to, such as tumours and cysts. There are many issues that might not start as a big problem, but become serious problems if not treated on time.

You should also never ignore any symptom that you see because an ignored symptom will lead to serious problems later. As in humans, an early detected problem or disease can be treated easily in cockroaches also.

The various diseases that your pet cockroach can suffer from are as follows:

Tumours and cysts

Your pet is also at risk of various cysts and tumours. If you notice any bumps on the body of the cockroach, don't take it lightly. This can be dangerous.

It occurs because of the uncontrolled growth of the cells in the cockroach's body. Though this is very common in these animals, it can be difficult to detect, especially in the earlier stages.

It is known that older cockroaches are more at risk of such tumours and cysts. But, various tumours can also attack younger cockroaches.

You should never take any symptom lightly and should visit the veterinarian when you observe changes in a cockroach. The veterinarian will conduct tests on the blood sample of the pet to confirm this health condition.

You can look out for the various common symptoms in the cockroach to know that he is suffering from this particular disease. You will notice sudden and drastic weight loss in the pet.

You will notice the pet to be very lazy and lethargic. It will appear that he has no energy to do anything. The pet will have visible bumps and changes in the skin texture. The pet will suffer from diarrhoea. The lymph nodes of the pet will also be swollen.

Another symptom that could accompany this disease is tiredness. The pet will experience some difficulty in his breathing and will acquire extreme tiredness.

Treatment:

It is important that you take the pet to the veterinarian. He will be able to administer certain medicines and injections. The veterinarian might also suggest surgery.

It is very difficult to save the pet after he has been diagnosed with this a deadly tumour. Mostly, it gets detected in later stages, so the treatment becomes all the more difficult.

Because the symptoms of this disease are very general, it is suggested that you ask your veterinarian to conduct yearly tests for your pet.

This would help in detecting any issue in the very beginning, which makes it possible to treat it successfully.

Rotten skin

Cockroaches shed the skin around the arms frequently. This will cause small flaks or pieces to float in the water. If these pieces are not removed, it can lead to rotten skin. The skin of the cockroach can also get infected by the bacteria on these skin pieces.

Cockroaches tend to suffer from the issue of dry skin. Dry skin is categorised by flaky skin. Some people mistake it for an infestation of algae.

If you attempt to look through the glass of the aquarium, you may see dry and loose flakes of skin. This is the main test of dry skin. There are a few causes that can lead to dry skin, such as improper diet and dry surroundings.

Treatment:

You can use olive oil capsules or vitamin E oil. These oils are easily available in all health stores. You can also put two to three drops in his food or water tank.

Continuous use of good quality oil will show you excellent results in a few weeks. Pour two to three drops of the oil at least once a week in the water tank of the pet.

It is also highly advised that you buy a mist humidifier. This will keep the water warm and humidity up. When a cockroach experiences low humidity levels, he can easily get dry skin.

If the problem does not end after all these measures, it is advised to get a skin scrape done by the veterinarian. This will help you to determine if there is more to the problem than what you understand.

Bacterial or fungal infection

Your cockroach can also be infected by yeast, bacterial or fungal infection. This can be very lethal so proper care should be taken.

In case you find the yeast infection symptoms, you should make it a point to take your pet to the vet. He will perform a stain test and confirm the presence or absence of the disease.

Causes:

There are many causes of the infection. The various causes that could be behind this health condition in your pet animal are as follows:

- Your cockroach can be infected by a yeast, bacterial or fungal infection. This can be very lethal so proper care should be taken.

- One of the main causes of any infection in cockroaches is lack of a healthy diet.

- If your animal is on oral antibiotics, then it will have some side effects on the body of the cockroach. This infection could be one of the side effects of the oral antibiotics.

- Another common cause of this health condition in cockroach is stress. When your pet animal is going through excessive stress, it will lead to this health condition.

- If there is poor hygiene around the cockroach, it can also lead to this health condition of infection. You should try to maintain optimum hygiene levels at all times.

- If the cockroach is suffering from some other infection or health condition, this infection could be a side effect of the health condition.

Symptoms:

There are certain symptoms that will help you to diagnose whether your cockroach has a yeast infection or not. In case you find the yeast infection symptoms, you should make it a point to take your pet to the vet. He will perform a gram stain test and confirm the presence or absence of the disease.

The following symptoms will help you to confirm whether your pet cockroach is suffering from this yeast infection:

- Do you smell something foul near your pet? If the answer is yes, then this could be the yeast infection.

- One of the early symptoms of this disease includes diarrhoea. If your pet is suffering from diarrhoea that you are not able to control, then your pet could be infected by this health condition.

- You should keep a check on the stools of the cockroach. The colour and texture of the stools will help you determine whether the cockroach has a yeast infection or not.

- Does your cockroach suffer from frothy stools? Is the stool dark yellow or green in colour? If yes, then this could be a clear case of a yeast infection or thrush.

- As the disease will progress, you will see more symptoms resurface. The mouth of the cockroach can get very sore and dry.

- Another symptom that you will notice as the disease spreads is lesions. You should be on the lookout for this particular disease.

Treatment:

If your cockroach is suffering from thrush, you don't need to worry as it can be treated. It is advised to administer 0.1 ml dose of antibiotic per one kilogram weight of the cockroach. Nilstat will effectively treat this yeast infection.

This is the dosage that is generally advised to treat most infections. You can even consult your veterinary before you give the dose to your pet.

When you are providing the treatment, there are certain precautions you need to take.

- After administering medicine, the pet might suffer from diarrhoea for a few days. This state can typically last for 2-3 days. Make sure that you take care of the pet's diet during this time because that will help him to revive from diarrhoea.

- The best way to administer medicine to the cockroach is to give each dose in between his feeds. This is the best way to help him fight against the diarrhoea.

- Another point that needs to be remembered is that you should never give the dose of medicine with the food that you serve the cockroach. There are many people who dissolve the dose in the water itself. This is not the right way because this will kill all the nutrition. The cockroach's health will only be harmed if you do something like this.

Adrenal disease

Adrenal disease occurs when the adrenal gland in the body malfunctions. A Madagascar hissing cockroach is prone to this disease. The main cause is growth of cells on a gland called the adrenal gland. This growth can present on the left or the right adrenal gland.

The growth on the gland can be both non-cancerous and cancerous. Though both the adrenal glands can possess such a growth, but it is said that the left gland is more prone to this disease than the right one.

It is generally noticed that Madagascar hissing cockroaches at the age of 3-4 years suffer from this disease. But, in many cases Madagascar hissing cockroaches below the age of three have also known to suffer from the adrenal disease.

One of the major effects of adrenal disease is a change in the hormonal production of the Madagascar hissing cockroach. This can often mislead many people. A drastic change in hormonal characteristics and production is often associated with Cushing's disease. But, this disease does not affect Madagascar hissing cockroaches.

Another problem with the diagnosis of the adrenal disorder is that the blood reports will be normal for the Madagascar hissing cockroach, indicating that all is fine with the animal. Even the X-ray reports will not show any issue. With changing times, technology has advanced.

There are some special blood tests that can be done for the Madagascar hissing cockroaches to diagnose the adrenal disorder. You should make sure that your veterinarian has the facility to consult these specialized blood tests.

It is important to understand that there are still many places and vets that don't have the facility to conduct these blood tests. In these cases, you will have to depend on the diagnosis of your veterinarian.

It is important that your veterinarian has the expertise to treat Madagascar hissing cockroaches. This will help him to read the symptoms correctly.

The exact cause for this disease is still not known. Though various tests are being done, the exact cause of adrenal disease still remains to be known. According to one theory, the spaying and neutering of Madagascar hissing cockroaches before they are sexually mature can lead to this condition.

There is another theory according to which the exposure to too much artificial lights can lead to this health condition in Madagascar hissing cockroaches. A Madagascar hissing cockroach is not very comfortable in extremely hot or cold temperatures. This is the reason that most owners keep their pet Madagascar hissing cockroach indoors.

Keeping the Madagascar hissing cockroach inside a room with artificial sources of light disrupts the natural cycle of the pet to a great extent. The artificial lights can lead to this malfunctioning of the adrenal gland. Another reason behind this condition is high stress levels in Madagascar hissing cockroaches.

You should try to keep your Madagascar hissing cockroach away from too much exposure to artificial lights. It is not possible to completely break the natural cycle of the pet, but there are a few precautions that you can take. The cage of the Madagascar hissing cockroach should have no source of artificial light.

In the evening time or when the weather is pleasant, you should take the pet out in the open. Allow him to play in a safe area. This will expose him to some natural light. Also, when he is indoors, you can make sure that he is exposed to dull lights.

You should not keep the Madagascar hissing cockroach in the dark and stress him out, just try to expose him to dull lights rather than exposing him to very bright artificial lights. The room should be exposed to the natural light cycles. It should not be artificially lit all the time.

You should also try to keep the stress levels of the Madagascar hissing cockroach to a bare minimum. Don't put him in the cage at all times. Let him be in a Madagascar hissing cockroach proof room of the house and also allow him to play in the open spaces of the house.

Symptoms:

Because the diagnosis of this disorder can be difficult, it makes it all the more important to read the symptoms well. You can look out for the following symptoms in the Madagascar hissing cockroach to know that he is suffering from this particular disease:

- You will notice sudden and drastic weight loss in the pet.

- There will be visible hair loss in the pet. If you observe the pattern of the hair loss, you will understand that it starts from the area of the tail. The hair loss moves up from there to the back of the animal.

- The skin of the Madagascar hissing cockroach can get very flaky. You will also notice that the skin appears itchy and it would develop sores with time.

- Males and females can show some unique symptoms also. For example, you might notice that the male is very active during mating and otherwise he shows lethargy in his movements and actions.

- The female Madagascar hissing cockroach will also show certain symptoms that can help you to diagnose this health condition. For example, the volva of the female will be swollen because of the growth on the adrenal glands.

Treatment:

In some cases, the animal is kept on a strict dose of certain medication. But, it should be noted here that this is not the permanent cure for the adrenal disease. This will definitely help to control the symptoms, but this is not a permanent cure.

If you wish to cure the pet fully then the effected part of the adrenal gland will have to be removed from the animal's body. After this, medication would have to be provided to help the other part of the gland to recover and function properly.

The disease and its treatment can have complications depending on the kind of tumour and also on the location of the tumour. If the outgrowth is cancerous, it automatically complicates the surgery. A metastasized tumour presents difficulties of removal, which complicates the process.

Also, if the affected adrenal gland is the left one, then the surgery is relatively simpler than when the right one is affected. The surgery on the right gland poses a danger to the major vena cava because the two are placed together.

There is a danger of rupturing the vein. If the entire right gland is not operated upon, then the symptoms can return.

Insulinomas

Low blood sugar condition in Madagascar hissing cockroaches leads to a condition called Insulinomas. When the Madagascar hissing cockroach develops a condition in which he has an abnormal growth over his pancreas that release insulin, it is referred to as Insulinomas.

The release of this insulin in the blood stream leads to a condition of low blood pressure or hypoglycaemia in the animal.

It is also important to note that these growths could either be cancerous or non-cancerous in nature. If the condition is not treated, it can get very serious and can even lead to the animal's death. A Madagascar hissing cockroach of more than three years of age is susceptible to this disease.

You should be on the lookout for the energy levels of the Madagascar hissing cockroach. If he sleeps more than his usual sleeping hours and is lethargic, you should know that something is wrong. Talk to his veterinarian and get his blood test done.

The exact cause of this health condition is still not known. But, in most cases it has been noticed that this disease either accompanies or follows the adrenal disease.

Because this disease is related to the pancreas, this condition is definitely affected by the kind of simple carbohydrates the pet is fed.

The high amount of sugar in the diet of the Madagascar hissing cockroach could also be a precursor to the disease. It is often advised that a Madagascar hissing cockroach should be served with a protein rich diet.

You should limit the carbohydrates and sugar and increase the amount of proteins in the pet's diet. Even the treats that are served to the pet Madagascar hissing cockroach should be healthy and not just sugar candies.

If you don't provide adequate amounts of protein in the diet of the animal, you will see him suffering from many ailments. There is no proof that a high protein diet can help you to avoid this condition, but it will definitely help in the Madagascar hissing cockroach's growth and development.

Symptoms:

You can look out for the following symptoms in the Madagascar hissing cockroach to know that he is suffering from this particular disease:

- You will notice the Madagascar hissing cockroach to be very lazy and lethargic. It will appear that he has no energy to do anything.

- He will sleep a lot. If you try to wake him up, he can be unresponsive.

- Your pet will experience disorientation. He will not feel or seem coordinated in his actions or movements.

- The Madagascar hissing cockroach will drool around the mouth and might also vomit occasionally. The pet will lose his appetite and will not show any interest in eating his food. He might also detest his favourite foods.

- Another symptom that can help you understand that your pet is suffering from Insulinomas is that he will experience seizures. You will notice sudden and jerky movements in the limbs of the pet. This could be accompanied by sudden passage of urine. He can also make sounds while he is sleeping.

Treatment:

One of the first things that you need to do when you see the pet suffering from a seizure is to apply Karo syrup all over. This syrup will help the pet to come out of a seizure that is related to hypoglycaemia.

But, application of the Karo syrup is by no means a permanent fix to the Madagascar hissing cockroach's problem. This is only a temporary relief to the poor pet.

Even after the temporary relief, you can expect another seizure very soon. This is because of the increased production of insulin in the Madagascar hissing cockroach. You should visit the veterinarian as soon as possible to get the Madagascar hissing cockroach tested. The vet will also give medication of Prednisolone to make sure that the blood sugar is stabilized.

He might also suggest surgery to operate on the growth on the pancreas. But, a major problem is that Insulinomas can reoccur. There is no permanent cure for this health condition.

Another complication that can arise from Insulinomas is that it can spread from the pancreas to other organs. This can be very detrimental to the Madagascar hissing cockroach's health.

In most cases, the vet advises surgery and continued medication for the pet. You would also have to ensure that you feed the pet with high protein and low carbohydrates in his meals. He should be fed frequent meals.

5. Taking care of a sick pet Madagascar hissing cockroach

If your Madagascar hissing cockroach is sick, then it is very important that you take him to a qualified veterinarian. It is never advised to self-medicate. For example, if your Madagascar hissing cockroach is suffering from fever and you decide to give the animal a medicine that you take for fever, then you are in for a shock.

The medicines that work on human beings or other animals might not necessarily work on your Madagascar hissing cockroach. You should never take this chance. Always consult the veterinarian before administering any medicine to the pet.

Along with the medication, you should also pamper the sick Madagascar hissing cockroach. Madagascar hissing cockroaches love to be loved and pampered. You will see them recovering fast when you give them your attention and care.

While it will be a little difficult for you to take care of the Madagascar hissing cockroach when he is sick, the experience can actually strengthen the bond that you share with the pet Madagascar hissing cockroach.

The first sign that something is not right with the Madagascar hissing cockroach is the body temperature of the animal. He should ideally be around 102 degree C. You should check this.

If you feel that the Madagascar hissing cockroach is very warm to touch, then you should know that the pet is not well.

Other symptoms that can help you to know that the pet is unwell include a lazy and lethargic pet. If you feel that the pet is not himself and has been acting very lazily, then this could be because he is unwell.

When you see the symptoms of a high fever in the pet, the first thing that you should do is make sure that the pet is drinking water. He can be given Pedialyte to help him recover. You should consult a veterinarian if the temperature does not come down in a few hours.

It is very important that you don't ignore the health condition of the Madagascar hissing cockroach. Even if he has a slight fever, you should take it seriously because before you know it, the slight fever can take shape of a life threatening disease. So, never hesitate to consult a vet in case of any doubts.

After you have consulted the veterinarian, you will have to spend a lot of time with your pet while he is recuperating from his illness. This can get very daunting for a new owner because he would not want to commit a mistake while taking care of his beloved pet.

You can take some simple precautions to make sure that your pet is healing better and faster. These precautions will ensure that the pet is getting all that is required for his healing process.

To begin with, you should always make sure that the pet is warm and comfortable. The pet will require something to curl into. He will also need his privacy at this time. Make sure that the Madagascar hissing cockroach has a blanket or shirt that will allow him to do so.

Do not force him to do anything that he does not want to. The pet needs some time and space. You should allow him to rest for as long as he wants. This will help him to heal in a better way.

If you have more than one Madagascar hissing cockroach, then you need to keep the sick pet isolated. This is to give the ill pet time to get better and to avoid spreading the disease.

If there are things and toys that the pets share, you should wash these things nicely and keep them separately. You should wash the bedding and other washable accessories in the cage of the Madagascar hissing cockroach.

A pet recovering surgery should be kept in a safe and closed environment so that he does not bruise himself.

A Madagascar hissing cockroach can get dehydrated very easily. The pet might throw up when he is not well. This can easily lead to dehydration. The Madagascar hissing cockroach will get disoriented if he is dehydrated for too long. You need to keep a check on the pet to ensure that he is not dehydrated.

You should make sure that the pet is drinking enough water to get better. But, in some cases the pet might just refuse to drink any water. The vet might also suggest intravenous injections in severe cases.

You should make sure that that the pet does not consume cold water. This can cause severe diarrhoea in the pet. Water at room temperature is the best for the Madagascar hissing cockroach.

If the Madagascar hissing cockroach is extremely dehydrated, you can serve him Pedialyte with water to help him get better. In severe cases, you can also give them Gatorade and water, but Gatorade needs to be diluted with larger quantities of water because of its high sugar content.

These fluids will help the Madagascar hissing cockroach to recover faster. Along with these mixes, your pet Madagascar hissing cockroach should have access to simple water at all times.

The veterinarian will suggest the exact dosage of the mixes that your Madagascar hissing cockroach needs depending on his condition. But, in general he should have 15-20 millilitres of the mix in every four hours.

A sick Madagascar hissing cockroach will get dehydrated pretty soon, so it is important to replenish his body with the water and the lost salts. If you feel that the pet is not having enough water, you should consult your vet about the condition of the pet.

If the pet Madagascar hissing cockroach does not drink the mix on his own, you will have to find a way to make him drink it. You can't force the pet, so the best way to replenish his body during a dehydration phase is to syringe feed him. If you take all the precautionary methods, this is not a difficult method.

To syringe feed the animal, take a clean syringe and fill it with the drink mix. Now, take this syringe to the side of the mouth of the pet. Slowly release a drop at a time in his mouth.

The Madagascar hissing cockroach will not be so easy to feed, so you need to be patient. You need to be careful so that the Madagascar hissing cockroach does not develop an infection.

The pet is not well, so you have to be prepared for making an extra effort for him at this time. No matter how much the pet resists, you have to make sure that he is being well fed when he is recuperating. You should also make sure that the pet is eating a nutritious diet to allow his body to heal quickly.

A sick pet will also lose interest in eating his food. You might have to take out time and hand feed him. You can use canned food or baby food that is prescribed by the veterinarian.

It is important that the food is easy on his digestive system. The sick pet needs nutrition, but does not need the pressure of digesting heavy foods. If the food is difficult for the digestive system of the Madagascar hissing cockroach to break down, it will lead to more complications.

Make sure that the food is not very hot or cold. It should be warm and just right for the Madagascar hissing cockroach.

Chapter 8: Grooming the Madagascar hissing cockroach

When you decide to keep a Madagascar hissing cockroach as a pet, you should understand that you will have to pay attention to the basic cleaning and grooming of the Madagascar hissing cockroach. This is essential to keep the Madagascar hissing cockroach clean and healthy. Not only will your Madagascar hissing cockroach appear neat and clean, he will also be saved from many unwanted diseases.

When you are looking at grooming sessions for your Madagascar hissing cockroach, you should pay special attention to the Madagascar hissing cockroach's bathing. This chapter will help you to understand the various dos and don'ts while grooming your pet Madagascar hissing cockroach.

1. Bathing the Madagascar hissing cockroach

Madagascar hissing cockroaches belong to the class of animals that are not extremely fond of bathing. Even within the Madagascar hissing cockroaches, there are some Madagascar hissing cockroaches that are okay with being in water and there are others who are hydrophobic. You will have to figure out whether your Madagascar hissing cockroach is hydrophobic or not.

If your Madagascar hissing cockroach is scared of water, you will have to try some tricks to get the Madagascar hissing cockroach clean. Even if the Madagascar hissing cockroach is hydrophobic, he needs to take a bath. This is something that you as the owner need to remember. The case of the hydrophobic Madagascar hissing cockroach will be discussed later in this section.

It will be a difficult task for you to bathe your pet. But, this is no way means that it is okay for the Madagascar hissing cockroaches to go without bathing. If the pet is not clean, he will attract fleas and other parasites. This only means extra work for you and veterinary visits for the Madagascar hissing cockroach.

To avoid the Madagascar hissing cockroach from getting sick, make sure that the Madagascar hissing cockroach is bathed every now and then. The frequency would depend on the climate and the environment of the Madagascar hissing cockroach. If it is too hot or if the surroundings are not too clean, it means that your pet should be given a bath more often.

Bathing is also important when the Madagascar hissing cockroach is recuperating from an illness. When you give the Madagascar hissing cockroach a bath, the dust and dirt will just get washed off with water. This also means that the dirt will not be shed all over the house.

Another point that you need to remember here is that while it is important to bathe the Madagascar hissing cockroach once in a while, over-bathing is not recommended. This can also create many problems. The skin of the Madagascar hissing cockroach will begin to lose many important essential oils if they are bathed frequently.

You will be surprised to learn this, but too much bathing can also increase the odour that the Madagascar hissing cockroach might emit. To save yourself from these issues, try to keep things under control. As a rule, give your Madagascar hissing cockroach a bath once in three or four weeks.

When you are looking to give a nice bath to your Madagascar hissing cockroach, you should be looking at two things, a good quality mild shampoo and a few towels. It is very important that you choose the right shampoo for the Madagascar hissing cockroach. If the shampoo is too hard or harsh, it might cause serious damage to his skin.

You can buy a good quality cat shampoo or a baby shampoo for the Madagascar hissing cockroach. These shampoos are very mild on the skin and have proven to be ideal for a Madagascar hissing cockroach. You also need a few towels handy for the Madagascar hissing cockroach. While one will be used to dry the water off, the others are required to cover the ground or floor.

If your Madagascar hissing cockroach is not scared of water then it will relatively easier for you to bathe it. But, even if it is there are a few precautions that you need to take. You should understand that how your Madagascar hissing cockroach behaves under water will depend on its individual personality.

It is important that you make a few attempts to understand your pet's personality. Don't give up and understand his behaviour and mannerisms. This will only help you in your future dealings with the pet.

To begin with, make sure that the water you are using to bathe the pet is warm. Madagascar hissing cockroaches have a body temperature that is different from human beings. They should be bathed in warm water to keep them safe.

Take a tub and fill it half with warm water. Lift your Madagascar hissing cockroach delicately in your hands. Make sure that your grip is firm. The Madagascar hissing cockroach might surprise you when it touches water and might try to jump out of your hands. To avoid such a situation, place your hands on the stomach area and hold him firmly.

Place the Madagascar hissing cockroach in the tub of warm water for a few seconds. Observe how he responds to water. If you see him enjoying, then your work becomes easier. You can also sprinkle water over the Madagascar hissing cockroach. But, if the pet Madagascar hissing cockroach is not enjoying then you need to be quick.

Another way to bathe your naughty hydrophobic Madagascar hissing cockroach is to sway him under running warm water. Turn the tap on and make sure the water is warm. It should not be cold or too hot. Once you are convinced that the temperature of the water is right for the pet, hold the pet and bring him under the water for a few seconds.

Keep him on the towels and use another towel to pat him dry. Make sure that he is absolutely dry before you let him go, otherwise dust and dirt will stick on his skin.

Conclusion

Thank you again for purchasing this book!

I hope this book was able to help you in understanding the various ways to domesticate and care for Madagascar hissing cockroaches.

Madagascar hissing cockroaches are adorable and lovable animals. These animals have been domesticated for many years. Even though they are loved as pets, they are not very common, and there are still many doubts regarding their domestications methods and techniques. There are many things that the prospective owners don't understand about the animal. They find themselves getting confused as to what should be done and what should be avoided.

A Madagascar hissing cockroach is a small naughty animal that will keep you busy and entertained by all its unique antics and mischiefs. It is said that each animal is different from the other. Each one will have some traits that are unique to him. It is important to understand the traits that differentiate the Madagascar hissing cockroach from other animals. You also have to be sure that you can provide for the animal. So, it is important to be acquainted with the dos and don'ts of keeping the Madagascar hissing cockroach.

If you are still contemplating whether you want to domesticate the Madagascar hissing cockroach or not, then it becomes all the more important for you to understand everything regarding the pet very well. You can only make a wise decision when you are acquainted will all this and more. When you are planning to domesticate a Madagascar hissing cockroach as a pet, you should lay special emphasis on learning about its behaviour, habitat requirements, diet requirements and common health issues.

The ways and strategies discussed in the book are meant to help you get acquainted with everything that you need to know about Madagascar hissing cockroaches. You will be able to understand the unique antics of the animal. This will help you to decide whether the Madagascar hissing cockroach is suitable to be your pet. The book teaches you simple ways that will help you to understand your pet. This will allow you take care of your pet in a better way. You should be able to appreciate your pet and also care well for the animal with the help of the techniques discussed in this book.

Thank you and good luck!

References

http://www.nationalgeographic.com

www.ehow.co.uk

http://www.mnn.com

https://en.wikipedia.org

https://www.lovethatpet.com

http://www.Madagascar hissing cockroach-world.com

https://www.bluecross.org.uk

http://www.seniorlink.co.nz

http://www.drsfostersmith.com

https://www.cuteness.com

http://www.vetstreet.com

https://www.hillsborovet.com

www.training.ntwc.org

http://animaldiversity.org

https://www.yourpetspace.info

https://www.finecomb.com

https://a-z-animals.com

https://www.theguardian.com

http://www.businessinsider.com

http://www.kijiji.ca

http://www.marshallpet.com

www.ingramcontent.com/pod-product-compliance
Lightning Source LLC
Chambersburg PA
CBHW060120050426
42448CB00010B/1964